CASUALTIES
OF
PEACEMAKING

A MEMOIR BY

BEVERLY JOHNSON BIEHR

the Peppertree Press

Sarasota, Florida

For information regarding permission,
call 941-922-2662 or contact us at our website:
www.peppertreepublishing.com or write to:
the Peppertree Press, LLC.
Attention: Publisher
1269 First Street, Suite 7
Sarasota, Florida 34236

ISBN: 978-1-61493-521-6

Library of Congress Number: 2017908786

Printed July 2017

DEDICATION

To my sons Luis and Juan
To all teenagers and twenty-thirty somethings
looking for life purpose
To all Vietnam veterans, welcome home!
To all Vietnam war protesters, peace!
To everyone who lived through the years 1968 to 1970
and still wonders

ACKNOWLEDGMENTS

The Florida Writers Association, writers helping writers, especially Lyn Hill, Sylvia Fiorello, and Carol Jones patiently coaxed this book from memory to memoir. Matt Peters pointed the way to the last re-write and a Royal Palm Literary Award. I met Julie Ann James of Peppertree Press at an FWA annual conference.

Chicagoan Laura A.M. Johnson contributed her story, as well as my best friend and one sister who were my roommates. Many other Chicagoans who became part of my life will recognize themselves on these pages, no matter what names they are given in my story.

Iowans Uncle Carl Johnson and brother Erwin Johnson contributed war stories. Sister Cindee Schnekloth had the idea of making the book user-friendly for book reading groups by creating a questionnaire. Niece Amy Kaiko Kassab turned the theme of the book into a web site www. activepeacemission.com

Last but not least, Harry, my Chicagoan husband, persevered and didn't lose hope.

CONTENTS

CHAPTER 1

1968 Democratic Convention from a Lincoln Park Perspective

FRIDAY, AUGUST 23, 1968

Three black men wearing black leather jackets and black berets walked briskly out of Chicago's O'Hare Airport entrance. My assigned protector and mentor, Eduardo, jumped out of my car and opened the back door. The sullen trio slid in without saying a word to us. I turned the ignition on, getting ready to go. Then I saw what must have upset them—a tall middle-aged white man in a business suit and hat stood in front of the car overacting the detectives' role; he appeared to be writing down my license number. I expected him to come over to speak to me, but he turned his back and walked away. I wondered who he was and why in the world he didn't walk the twenty feet to my car window and talk to me directly.

When Eduardo got back in the passenger seat, he gave me strict instructions, "Drive a little under the speed limit. Concentrate on your driving. Give hand signals when you make a turn. Make sure you don't break any traffic laws."

I wasn't sure what to say, so I used a life lesson I once learned: When in doubt, don't! I kept my mouth shut and checked to make sure the passengers were seated in the back seat, then silently drove my two-tone black and white 1957 Ford Fairlane 300 toward the airport exit.

One of the men in the back seat asked Eduardo, "Whe' dis episode goin' down, bro?"

"Whadd'ya say?"

The man repeated his question. Sounding exasperated, Eduardo said, "Man, I can't understand you."

"Why the hell don't they give us someone who speaks English?"

I caught a glimpse of the infamous Bobby Seale in the rearview mirror. I swallowed hard, and in a moment of self-doubt, thought to myself—*Bev, you're a country girl from Iowa. Here you are—a brand-new resident of Chicago, Illinois. Are you sure you know what you're doing, escorting world-renowned Black Panther men down the Kennedy Expressway to a peace rally in Lincoln Park?*

Just then the same guy asked in totally understandable English, "Lady, can you tell me where we're going? Do you know?"

"I was told to take you to Lincoln Park—to a peace rally there."

"Ya know how to get there?"

"Yes."

He said no more to me, apparently satisfied with my answer. The three men went on talking in lowered tones among themselves. I heard them call the one, Bobby, so that confirmed for me that the man in the middle was Bobby Seale and the other two were probably his bodyguards. My Latino colleague leaned close to my ear and said in low tones in Spanish, "*Despues me dices lo que estan diciendo, okay?*" (Afterwards you tell me what they're talking about, okay?) I nodded.

We arrived at Lincoln Park, and saw the crowd in an open area just south of the Lincoln Park Zoo. People surrounded the car when I stopped, greeted the visitors, then hustled us all to a makeshift stage. Someone told me to stand behind Seale along with about fifteen other supporters of all races. He was introduced to the crowd as Bobby Seale, cofounder of the Black Panther Party for

Self-Defense from San Francisco. He started his speech proclaiming, "Power to the people!" The crowd cheered and applauded wildly and the exuberance continued after every other sentence about politicians jiving and making promises about ending war they had no intention of keeping. He guaranteed us that the power structure of this country was about to feel a new kind of politics that just won't quit! My heart was racing. I said aloud to the guy beside me, "Wow, this is a real peace rally!"

Once he paused for a moment until the crowd quieted down. His voice changed to teaching mode; he said that there were many pigs (policemen) just waiting for an excuse to take action against antiwar demonstrators. He encouraged the audience not to fear the "pigs" but to stand up to them, and not return violence for violence, unless necessary for self-protection. I looked out at the audience again and saw a menacing ring of policemen surrounding the crowd like the frame of a picture. He concluded by saying liberation was a righteous cause more important than anyone knows. "These antiwar demonstrations will be seen around the world! Power to the people!"

After his speech, one of the guys with Bobby Seale told me to take them to the SDS (Students for a Democratic Society) headquarters on the north side. When we got there, my passengers asked me to wait for them; they didn't know how long it would be, but after they were done there, they wanted to go to a friend's house on the South Side. I was dismayed, wondering how long I would have to wait there in the dark. After I translated their words into Spanish for Eduardo, he said to tell them, "No, tell them we have somewhere else to go."

I was pleasantly surprised that Seale said that would be okay and that they would find a ride. The Panther trio got out without another word and disappeared into the house. I didn't know then that I would see Bobby Seale again about six months later. And I would see that same "airport detective" even sooner.

As I headed back to the Armitage Avenue United Methodist Church in Lincoln Park where Eduardo and I were recruited for this amazing errand, I told him that I couldn't hear a lot of the Black Panthers' conversation when they were in my car, but Seale was in Chicago apparently as a replacement speaker for Eldridge Cleaver, a cofounder of The Black Panthers. I told him they commented about the huge police presence, making Chicago look more like a war zone than anything they had ever seen.

We talked about how we were recruited for the day's activities. Eduardo said he worked at the church part-time as a janitor. Today he was at the church to help a busload of war protestors get settled, since they were staying for the week of the Democratic Convention in the church basement. They came from Cleveland, Ohio, for antiwar demonstrations to try to get the Democrats to change their platform at the 1968 Democratic Convention and adopt a position to end the Vietnam War.

I told him I had worked in the church all summer as one of the summer school teachers in Mayor Daley's Peace Corps program, and my job was supposed to end just before the convention started. I was in the basement gathering up supplies and teaching materials. All of a sudden, the Ohio war protestors who had been busy unpacking their sleeping bags began mulling around frantically looking for people with cars. They were talking about a large number of Black Panthers arriving at the airport. They needed people with cars to go out to the airport to meet them and bring them to the peace rally in Lincoln Park. Their group couldn't help, because they had come by bus. When I told them I had a car, a small group materialized out of nowhere, cajoling me to help out the peace movement.

"That's what convinced me to volunteer. You know, Eduardo, my mom brought me up to always help anyone who needed it, if I could. I guess I obeyed her voice in my head."

Eduardo laughed. "Same with me. Pastor asked me to go with you, so you wouldn't be alone. He told me to give you those driving instructions."

"That's funny. I thought you were a big wig in the protest movement!"

"Far from it. I couldn't barely hear dos guys. Maybe my hearing's bad. I don't know what woulda happened if you didn't know what they were saying. It woulda been a disaster. How'd ya do it?"

I puzzled on that question for a moment and then I remembered. "One summer during college I worked in a camp for inner city kids in New York State. I was the camp dietitian working in a kitchen where the cooks were all from somewhere down south like South Carolina. They made some of the best food I ever ate in my life, but I had to listen well to understand them so I could order the ingredients they needed. I guess you never worked with southern blacks, huh?"

"Naw. Not yet anyway. I thought dos guys came from California."

"They did. But he sounded like he was from Texas or somewhere like that."

"Who knows? Wha'd ya think of Bobby Seale?"

"To tell the truth, he was handsome, but it was all kinda weird. They never once said hello or thank you. I wonder why?" I thought for a moment. "Maybe it was because I had my role; I was the driver. You had your role; you were like my body guard. Bobby Seale was the featured speaker. The other two were his body guards. As I'm talking, it's becoming clearer to me: it was like a routine business trip for them."

"And our church is right in the middle of all the commotion. This is a helluva place to be if you wanna be a war protester."

"Yeah, Lincoln Park is where the action is."

I dropped Eduardo off at the church, shaking hands and saying to each other, *"Mucho gusto en conocerle."* (Pleasure to meet you.)

On the way home, I couldn't help feeling sad that it was my last day on that summer job. It had been an eventful summer and I might never see the kids again. The planned war protests at the Democratic Convention put an abrupt end to our summer program. All we had left was the final teacher meeting. The pastor-director had called it for the next week after the Democratic Convention was over, and that's when we would get our final paychecks.

What I didn't tell Eduardo was that I was actually a war protestor, too. Just one evening prior, some of the Ohio war protestors staying in the church invited me and my fellow teachers to a nighttime training rally at Lincoln Park. Only Carlos, the art teacher, and I went with them. We listened to their chit chat as we walked ten blocks to Lincoln Park with them. "I think we have no business in Vietnam. People need to get louder to protest the war. I know I sure as hell don't want to go fight over there. Whatever we can do to reach the people who make the laws, we gotta do. We gotta stop this war. This beats sitting at home and twiddling my thumbs and complaining." I discovered I agreed with them, but I was in for a surprise.

Arriving in the park, we found a man barking orders on a megaphone while organizing a large group of people there to lock arms to form a human chain. He yelled at us to join in on the end. This was no childhood "Crack the Whip" game. As the men in the center started its circular movement, those of us on the end were practically pulled off our feet when the movement got to us.

The speaker gave us credit for being fast learners and pointed out the advantage of this resistance tactic was that it would mow down policemen or anyone else who got in our way. Then he announced that the next night's training would be on "shit," and we should bring some to practice ways to throw it effectively.

I thought I had heard him wrong at first. People around me laughed, but I was appalled. I expressed my feelings to Carlos on the walk back to the church.

"That isn't at all what I expected. I don't get it; why do they have to go to such extremes?"

"Ya know why? I heard tell that Mayor Daley gave orders to police to 'shoot to kill' anyone who tries to disrupt the Democratic convention. That's serious, Bev. A counterattack like we just practiced would only be used to stop police brutality."

"I'm not convinced. I think I'm gonna opt out of that kind of war protest. That stuff about throwing poop? I would never ever do that! And a human chain designed to injure policemen? Why? I don't think it would work anyway."

"Bev, I'm gonna tell you something. You gotta decide whose side you're on. If you're not for the revolution, then you're for the establishment."

"Revolution? Hey, I thought when they talk about revolution, they just mean lots of things gotta change in this country, but battling it out with police? No, thanks. Not for me."

Truthfully, I was in a quandary. I didn't want to join either side—violent revolution or the political establishment—but I couldn't articulate why. Questions raced through my mind. *Was I just a big chicken—afraid to commit myself to radical action to end the war? What else could one person do to get our government to end the war and the killing? What would happen to our country if there really were a revolution?*

That night after I got to the apartment and had a cup of coffee, my sister Rachel came home. We decided to spend the next week in Iowa instead of Chicago for various reasons. We had a one week break before we could get our final paycheck. Our parents were expecting us to come home after we finished our work for the summer. Rachel had to decide what was next for her and her fifteen-month-old son, Markie. I had a little more than one week to get ready for teacher orientation on my first teaching assignment in the Chicago Public School system. Mayor Daley's Peace Corps Program had been an amazing introduction to the city of Chicago and my first chance to work with Chicago youth; I felt that was enough for now. We decided to leave as soon as we could get out of the city the next day.

I was still all worked up about the events of the day, especially happy that things had worked out for me to help take Bobby Seale where he needed to go, so I drove back to the church to get my box of teaching supplies, which I had actually forgotten in all the excitement. I knew the church would be open, since the Ohio protesters would be returning from the rally in Lincoln Park. Sure enough, the basement was spread with sleeping bags, knapsacks, and duffle bags. The returning protesters were excited about their experiences at Lincoln Park. I found out they were members of a group called the Cleveland Area Peace Action Council, some on vacation from their jobs, some high school or college students waiting for fall classes to begin.

A lot of them were decrying the lack of media people covering the wonderful rally where Bobby Seale spoke. They were wondering what could be done to get newspaper reporters and photographers to cover their antiwar activities. All seemed committed to getting the word out and making a statement about ending the war, no matter what extremes they were going to have to take.

After loading up my box of teaching supplies, I drove home the twenty blocks along Halsted Avenue. I let my mind wander and imagined a thoughtful news reporter observing how our country was becoming seriously divided over the Vietnam War and related social issues, and feeling it necessary to present a balanced picture of the average antiwar demonstration. If by some remote chance a reporter had asked to interview me when I was there in Lincoln Park protesting the war, I thought about how the interview might have unfolded:

Question: Why are there so many war protesters here?

Answer: The government never made a good case with high school or college students as to why it was necessary to go to the other side of the world to fight against a country that never attacked our country. There was no Pearl Harbor. There was no declaration of war. Our generation is not one to blindly follow orders. We want reasonable explanations. There is a growing realization of the senselessness of the Vietnam War.

Question: What do you young war protesters talk about among yourselves?

Answer: We have many a discussion about important things. One of the main ones is how eighteen-year-olds can be sent to war and die, but they can't even vote. We all were required to take a government course in high school, but then we can't vote or participate in government decision-making for another three of four years until we're twenty-one. What are we supposed to do in the meantime—read about the war-crazed politicians in power? Furthermore, laws in most states deny us other adult privileges, such as marrying and drinking wine or beer. It seems as though everything we like is put down, such as rock and roll, or illegal, such as pot smoking. How else can we let it be known how unfair the laws are but through group protests?

Question: This sounds like a classic generation gap. Is it?

Answer: It might be. I think my parents' attitude toward arbitrary laws like making up a special park curfew for the Democratic Convention would be the same as mine. But no, I think it is more than that. I think the media has been unfairly portraying demonstrators as empty-headed vagrants, pot smokers, and sex maniacs. Instead, you can see who we really are, at least here in the Midwest. We're mainly working class young people and college students protesting the endless Vietnam War.

Question: Are you primarily protesting the war or protesting the laws on how you are treated here in the USA?

Answer: There's a lot to protest, but the war is about life and death. It doesn't seem as though our leaders took our country into this war to win. The Korean conflict was another senseless war during our lifetimes. As far as I can see, our country went and fought on the other side of the globe for a while, spent lots of money on weapons, sent our older brothers off to die, and then quit. The 38th parallel was drawn as a compromise, but it separated families and a culture. Is the war in Vietnam any different? We need to ask ourselves: what would "winning" look like? Is there a way to win? Is there any intention of winning? Or is our country again fighting a war so there can be a military industry to enrich the already rich? We war protesters feel there are no good reasons given for being aggressors in civil wars in other parts of the world.

I knew I was just one person and my experiences of the important events that were happening in Chicago and in the nation were unique, but one thing I had in common with the other protesters was that I had very little time to reflect on my role in all of this. By default, we were letting the media define us. Reporters and photographers were taking the easy way to make news interesting; they were searching for any violent incidents and showing the bizarre, rather than presenting all sides in order to get to the truth. Once I appreciated the media bias for violence, I understood why the war protesters were planning for confrontations with police.

I wondered, *Will future generations believe the prevalent lie that we 1960s war protestors were no more than a bunch of troublemakers, rabble-rousers, drug addicts, and lazy and unemployed hippies without a serious thought in our heads?* I began to realize that those of us who were activists needed to tell our own stories; otherwise, this portion of our nation's history might be lost. I resolved to do that one day.

As it turned out, the protest rally that I attended on Friday night was the most peaceful demonstration of the entire week. Bobby Seale was scheduled to speak again the next day in downtown Grant Park and that is when police and protesters first clashed. He was invited to stay and speak the next week in Grant Park. Those speeches were taped, as opposed to the one I attended Friday night, when there was apparently no media coverage. (Seale, Bobby. *A Lonely Rage: The Autobiography of Bobby Seale.* New York: Times Books, a NYT Book Company, 1978.)

However, Mayor Daley expected the worst and prepared well. "The usual police contingent of 6,000 officers on the streets grew to 11,900 on twelve-hour shifts, up from the usual eight. The city requested the mobilization of 5,649 Illinois National Guardsmen, with an additional 5,000 on alert, bolstered by up to 1,000 Federal Bureau of Investigation (FBI) officers and military intelligence officers. Waiting for signs of trouble in the suburbs would be 6,000 army troops, including members of the elite 101st Airborne Division—police helicopters patrolled—looking for any sign of trouble." (Kusch, Frank. *Battleground Chicago: The Police and the 1968 Democratic National Convention.* Chicago and London: The University of Chicago Press, 2008, pg. 53.)

Bobby Seale was right when he observed the overabundance of police presence. Mayor Daley made a public announcement to reassure the citizens of Chicago that all points of view were welcome during convention week; however, demonstrators should be aware that there would be no disruption allowed. The conditions that were set up to keep the peace actually made clashes between protesters and police inevitable.

CHAPTER 2
Mayor Daley's Peace Corps

SATURDAY, AUGUST 24, 1968

After we got started on the all-day drive from Chicago to northern Iowa, my sister Rachel wanted to know why I went out to the airport. I told her I had been looking for a way to put my antiwar beliefs into action, so if I could support the protestors by picking up their main speaker and taking him to their first big rally, I thought at least it was something constructive.

Rachel said, "I never woulda done it if I were you, Bev. It was way too risky."

"They said they would get the pastor to send someone with me. He would meet the Panthers and he would do all the talking. All I had to do was drive."

"Is that how it worked out?"

"Well, no, he didn't know 'em either. He was the church janitor. I ended up being a translator between him and the Black Panthers. Apparently his English wasn't good enough to understand the way blacks talk sometimes."

"I had some trouble understanding 'em at first, too. How did you get so good?"

"The janitor, Eduardo, asked me that, too. Don't you remember that summer job I had between my junior and senior year at college working in a camp with inner city kids from New York? I worked in the kitchen with cooks from down south all summer. They really had heavy accents. I remember how I had to ask them to repeat what they were saying to me over and over until I finally understood. We got to laughing about it, but I think they liked me, because they knew I was trying."

Rachel was silent for a moment. "I wish I woulda done what you did and went to other states to work while I was in college. I always stayed home to help Mom around the house."

"Well, that's okay, sis. Just different. I couldn't resist the urge I'd always had as long as I can remember to get out and see the world. I loved living in Iowa, but I got to spend my summers in camps in Michigan, Colorado, and New York State." I smiled at the memories while keeping my eyes on the road. We were still in the outer suburbs of Chicagoland, but traffic was getting lighter.

"That's probably why you weren't afraid to go meet the Black Panthers from California. I was afraid for you, but I shoulda known you could handle yourself around blacks. What about that John character that keeps calling you on the phone?"

"He's just a friend. I haven't seen him all summer. We were too busy."

"Are you gonna tell the folks?"

"Tell 'em what?" I was starting to get defensive.

"That you've gone out on dates with a black guy?"

"No, why should I tell them?"

"Look, I don't want to start a fight or anything, but you shouldn't be doing things like that, Bev."

"Why not? He's just a different skin color, that's all."

"It's a lot more than that and you know it."

I kept my eyes on the highway, gritting my teeth. "I suppose you are going to tell the folks, so you might as well know the truth.

I worked with him at Michael Reese Hospital. I went to a party or two with him, that's all."

"Are you sure that's all?"

"Yes, that's all." I knew I wasn't a good liar, but it was safer to keep trying. "You were with me all summer. Did you see anything else? Listen, let's talk about something else, or I'm gonna quit talking."

Rachel was silent for a moment. "So what happened out at the airport?"

I breathed a sigh of relief. This was a safer topic.

"I parked the car in the passengers' drop-off area and left it there while Eduardo and I went inside. There at the terminal gate pacing the floor was none other than Abby Hoffman. I recognized him by his long Afro style hair. Eduardo talked to him and told them who we were. He told us that we had better go back out to the car and wait, or they might tow my car away."

Rachel asked, "So what was going on in Lincoln Park then? Was it pretty wild?"

"No, the whole rally in Lincoln Park was totally peaceful. There was a big crowd and they cheered and clapped for Bobby Seale constantly. I was standing right behind him. Lots of cops were in position around the perimeter of the crowd. I'm glad I was there, but I'm glad I'm going home now."

"I didn't bargain for the Democratic Convention and all the war protesters when I told you I would take the summer job." My younger sister yawned sleepily. "The whole summer was kinda overwhelming, wasn't it? I am just glad we made it safely through all the classes with the kids."

"I guess that's one of the main differences between us two 'schwesters.'" I smiled, but I was serious. "You get all emotional about things, Rachel. I don't. Usually I don't even notice my feelings

21

until afterwards, if at all. It's probably not too good for me, because sometimes I get stomach aches when I keep everything inside."

"Well, the only reason I came to work with you this summer was because I trusted you, Bev. Even though you're only two years older, you're the rock as far as I'm concerned." She sounded more conciliatory.

"I'm not all that solid. I make plenty of mistakes just like everyone else, but at least I'm in there trying. I'm glad you took the risk of coming to Chicago to work. We did a good thing this summer, sis. Listen, instead of tattle telling to the folks, let's tell 'em about our job adventures in Mayor Daley's Peace Corps Program."

I made sure I got on the right highway, the one headed to Iowa, instead of Wisconsin. Rachel responded, "It was one amazing summer with those Chicago teenagers. Yeah, let's only talk with the folks about the summer program. I know Mom and Dad will be interested." I took in a breath of relief.

Finally in agreement, we both broke into our family's old favorite traveling song, "Oh, I'm from I-O-way, I-O-way, state of all the land, corn on every hand. Oh, I'm from Iowa, Iowa, that's where the tall corn grows."

Rachel said she was going to take a nap. Her blond hair blowing in the breeze from the open windows, she looked at total peace with the world. She said quietly to no one in particular, "I'm so anxious to see my precious Markie. Thank goodness my baby boy could stay the summer with the folks. He sure loves his grandpa and grandma."

I rolled the car window down and stretched my left arm out, letting the wind blow noisily against my fingers, arm and face, to celebrate the freedom of getting past the city and suburbs. I looked forward to the three-hundred-mile road trip from Chicago across northern Illinois to north central Iowa. My father had warned me that the six-cylinder Ford Fairlane 300 would have trouble getting up the hills around scenic Galena. So I planned to speed up and make a run for them, and as soon as the car shifted itself out of overdrive to third gear, I would prepare to shift down to second. I was quite sure that would work. Luckily, I had learned to drive on a stick shift. It seemed like a different world as the four-lane highway became two-lane highway by Rockford, and eventually, it would be a gravel road when we got to our farm home where Rachel and I grew up. Although I loved my life in the Chicago area where I had lived for almost three years, this transplanted country girl could still get homesick for fields of corn and oats stretching out as far as the eye could see. My sister fell asleep.

I let my mind wander back to the day I got the summer teaching job in Chicago. My job interview came by responding to a job announcement on the college bulletin board at the student center. I was completing my course work for a Master of Arts degree and needed some income so I could move to Chicago again and share an apartment with my friend, Janice. She was one of the gals with whom I had roomed when I first came to Chicago.

I remembered that beautiful sunny Friday in April 1968 walking through the Northwestern University campus to catch the Evanston Express commuter train to Chicago. Students were having a Vietnam War protest. I had never seen an antiwar demonstration, but I remembered thinking that this one was quite laid back, not like the ones in the newspapers. No angry march. No one lecturing from a soapbox. No rally. This protest was more like a sit-down strike. Hundreds of students were lounging on blankets on the lawn in front of the campus library, drinking soda pop, talking, and laughing. Two cars drove down Sheridan Road toward the northern suburbs, honking their horns. The passengers waved gaily out their windows, and student demonstrators were quick to respond, cheering and waving their homemade *Make Love - Not War* and *War No More* signs. I believed in peace, was against the Vietnam War, and had a little time to spare, so I decided to look for someone I knew. Finding no one familiar, I kneeled down beside a student sitting alone, idly strumming a guitar, and sang with him, "How many roads must a man walk down before they call him a man?" Indeed, I felt I was walking onto roads unknown on my way to adulthood. What I liked about this protest was that it was an open invitation all-campus get-together with a purpose—join a nationwide organization called Students for a Democratic Society (SDS) in their call to take a stand for peace and against the Vietnam War. And what a coincidence, that I was going to interview for a summer Chicago Peace Corps job.

During the thirty-minute train ride into Chicago, I tried to imagine my upcoming job interview. I believed I would be qualified for the job of teaching in Mayor Daley's summer youth program, because I would emphasize that I had an undergraduate college degree in secondary education and I was fluent in Spanish.

My interview was at the Armitage Avenue Methodist Church located about ten blocks west of Lincoln Park. As I walked in the front door, a sign on the wall in Japanese or Chinese caught my eye. I was curious and decided to ask my interviewers about it. I found the church office, but it was empty. Hearing voices in the basement, I headed down the stairs. There were two men engrossed in conversation in front of a window opening into a kitchen. One was a tall Anglo guy and the other a short Hispanic guy.

I decided to relive the job interview in my mind after I crossed the Mississippi River Bridge and got on Iowa soil.

24

"Hi, I'm Beverly Johnson. I have an interview for a summer job here."

The taller man said, "Well, isn't that something? I didn't expect a teenager. How old are you?"

"I'm older than you think. I'm 29 years old." I was used to being mistaken for five or even ten years younger than I was.

"Sorry for the inquisition. I'm a Johnson, too, Bruce Johnson, the senior pastor here, and this is Sergio Herrera, the assistant pastor. Do you want to know how old we are?"

"No, that's okay. You look old enough for your jobs." We all laughed.

"Actually we're all about the same age. Do you know anything about this summer program?"

"Not really. Is it something to keep kids busy and out of trouble?"

"Yes, but much more. It's called Mayor Daley's Peace Corps Program. Youth will be paid to take classes. The program is for Latinos in this church and there's a sister program for black youth in a Catholic-turned-Baptist Church south of here near the Cabrini Greens housing projects. The idea is that all the youth will take the same types of classes—them over there and us here. The whole purpose is empowerment. Have you heard the motto, 'Power to the people'?"

"I've heard it, but I'm not sure what it really means."

"It can mean lots of things, but this summer it means building self-esteem through learning about your own culture. Secondly, it means learning the Chicago political system and how to make it work for you. Have you heard of Saul Alinsky?"

"Yes, I have. He's a community organizer. My pastor, Reverend Neuman, talks a lot about Saul Alinsky and how he has taken his trainings. He always wants us church members to get involved in

25

doing things to protect and improve Humboldt Park."

"Right, I know Jim very well. We're friends in fact. How long have you gone to Humboldt Park Methodist Church?"

"Three years, since I came to the Chicago area. The only type of church I wanted to go to was a Spanish-speaking church after I had just finished working almost four years as a short-term Methodist missionary in Mexico. You probably know they have two congregations—one English and one Spanish."

"So you must be fluent in Spanish. That's interesting. Community organization is really needed in Latino communities here in Chicago. Organizing people to stand up for themselves and for each other is exactly what we call *Power to the People*."

Reverend Johnson stopped for a moment, scratched his head, and asked, "Do you have any teaching experience?"

"Yes, student teaching in Iowa and four years in a nurses' training school in Chihuahua, Mexico."

He nodded his head. "Yeah, you have the background for this summer job all right. But do you think you can handle inner-city kids?"

"I'd better learn since I'm in the process of applying to teach in the Chicago Public Schools."

"Very good. Do you know anyone else who could teach in this summer program?"

"Actually I do. My sister would like to come to Chicago for the summer. She's a teacher, too."

"Good. You're both hired. When can you start?"

"I can start right away. I'll have to contact my sister and find out when she can get here from Iowa."

He told me what day to report to work. I remembered to ask about the sign by the front door. Bruce explained that it was Japanese for, "You Are Welcome Here. You are Safe Here." He explained that during World War II the church sponsored Japanese Americans to work in Chicago who had been arrested on the west coast just for being Japanese, and sent to a "relocation camp" in Kansas. "It wasn't a pretty part of our national history," he said, "but with the help of this church, quite a number of individuals and families were released from custody even before the end of the war. The Japanese people that came to Chicago formed a faith community and called themselves 'Christian Fellowship.' " He explained that they met in this church for years until they outgrew the space and found a church building further north to call their own.

I wished I would have been able to meet some of those courageous old-timers, church members who saw the injustice of incarcerating people whose only "crime" was being Japanese-American when Japan, the country, became our mortal enemy during the war. I also wished to meet some of the Japanese Americans, and learn about their experiences. But that summer went by so fast and we were so busy with the young people, I never had a chance to pursue those desires.

I smiled to myself, feeling very fortunate that I had stumbled across such a justice-oriented place to work for a summer when my only intention was to make some much needed money. I knew for sure that getting to work with Chicago teenagers for a summer would be good preparation for my upcoming teaching job.

My life since I left the farm where I grew up had been one life-changing experience after another. I was painfully shy and naive when I first left home to enroll in Iowa State College. Being determined not to flunk out like some of the neighbor boys had, I overcame my fears, worked hard, and I did stick it out until I earned a degree four years later in home economics education with a minor in foods and nutrition. My next four years working as a Peace Corps style missionary, hospital dietitian, and nursing school instructor in Chihuahua, Mexico, I proved to myself that I could survive and thrive in another culture. I fell in love with Mexico and flirted with the idea of staying there after my contract ended. I probably would have stayed, if I had followed through with any of the marriage discussions I had with four different guys: a Chinese medical supplies salesman, a Mexican medical intern, a young Mexican doctor, and a Mexican musician. I even gave my violin to Humberto Hernandez, the musician who was starting a school of music in Culiacan. None of the relationships worked out, probably because of my fear of falling in love and making a commitment, but I was surprised how sad I felt when Herman Ramirez, the medical intern, broke up with me because he fell in love with someone else. I looked forward to returning to Chihuahua for a visit as soon as I could afford it.

This past spring I finished my coursework for a master's degree from Northwestern University/Garrett Seminary. All I lacked now was to take the comprehensive final written exam and oral exam to earn a Master of Arts degree from Northwestern University. I knew that preparation for the exams would entail a lot of reading and studying, and I wasn't sure I would ever get to it. My motivation was lacking ever since I had looked into church jobs and found there were very few for women. Women had been allowed to become pastors since 1956 in the Methodist Church, only twelve years ago, but the seminary told me that churches weren't really ready for women pastors yet, especially young single women like me. I had never known a woman pastor anyway. I did apply for a Christian Education job in Arlington Heights, a suburb of Chicago. They accepted me and told me that a nice church couple had a room they would rent me to live in. I told them that I intended to share an apartment with a friend in Chicago and I could commute out to Arlington Heights. They weren't in favor of that, saying they wanted their workers to live in the community; besides, no one commuted from Chicago to work in the suburbs. Their church members commuted from the suburbs to Chicago to work. I knew I had to follow my own dreams of living and working where the action was—in Chicago. And I said to myself, *If they don't want me the way I am, then I don't want them.*

I was glad I had to take time out from my two years of university studies to work one summer as a hospital dietitian in Presbyterian-St. Luke's Hospital and the next seven or eight months as a therapeutic dietitian in Michael Reese Hospital. Why? Because it helped me decide I wanted to stay on living and working in Chicago, and not to pursue a life-long career in dietetics. I knew it was the teaching part of my various jobs that I liked the best. Thank goodness, I had a teaching certificate from Iowa State College so after the suburban church job didn't work out, I applied to the Chicago Public Schools system. Part of the application process to teach in Chicago was to get the teaching certificate transferred from Iowa to Illinois. When I was interviewed in the Department of Home Economics, the director and two of the consultants were graduates of Iowa State. They said that anyone with a home economics degree from Iowa State would be an excellent teacher. I hoped they were right.

When my sister and I arrived at our Iowa home, our mother and father greeted us warmly and said supper was ready. We hugged and kissed little fifteen-month-old Markie, who laughed and basked in all the attention. I missed my younger sister, Sydnee, who had graduated from high school that spring and already left for college orientation. And brother, Erwin, was on the other side of the world in Laos working for International Voluntary Service in lieu of military service. I helped Mom put the hot food on the table. Our family had always eaten evening meals together, and that was a good time to talk. The menu was my favorite—pork chops, boiled potatoes, green beans, and salad, everything raised or grown on the farm as our family had always done. We all sat down around the dining room table and said grace.

As soon as everyone had served themselves, Mom told us they were anxious to hear about our summer's work in Mayor Daley's Peace Corps program, just as Rachel and I had anticipated. She especially wondered what kind of students we had. Rachel explained that one of the biggest challenges for her was that they spoke teenager talk in a combination of English and Spanish. Their Spanish was Puerto Rican Spanish which is spoken very fast with the last sounds of most words omitted. Rachel told how we all called each other by our first names. The director was Reverend Bruce Johnson and he wanted to be called Bruce, which seemed strange. She had always called pastors by their last names and students called teachers by last names.

I jumped in and explained that the students were paid minimum wage to participate in summer school and to paint the church basement and stairways. Bruce divided the youth into three groups; they rotated among mine and Rachel's classes, and there was one other teacher besides Rachel and me. Art and culture class was taught by Carlos Ortiz who was also in charge of the church painting assignment.

Rachel added that Carlos was a young Puerto Rican guy who graduated a year ago from Waller, the neighborhood high school. She imitated his voice. "Hey, man, ya gotta finish school; if I could do it, so can you." Rachel continued that she taught Puerto Rican history and since she only knew what she had written in a college paper, she did team teaching with Carlos, as they painted wall murals in the basement. She learned a lot about art and music, as she related them to history.

I told them my assignment was to teach Chicago government. The point was for the teenagers to learn how to influence and change city government eventually. Bruce was passionate about the fact that Chicago elections were coming up in the fall, and what a shame it was that there were no Puerto Rican aldermen in a city with one of the top five Puerto Rican populations on mainland USA. Furthermore, there were no Latino aldermen at all, and that included Mexicans, Central Americans, Cubans, and South Americans.

Dad asked, "How could that be? Don't Spanish people vote?"

I answered, "Well, that's gotta be the problem, but Bruce informed us that there are reasons. They don't have anyone to get motivated to vote for—other than Chicago machine candidates pre-selected in smoke-filled ward offices. Then the wards are gerrymandered to split the Hispanic vote. Bruce wanted me to figure out how to address issues like that in my classes, so I did."

We finished the meal, and took time to get homemade apple pie served for dessert. Mom reminded us she was a country school teacher before she was married. "Now we have three teachers in the family. I'm so proud of you girls teaching in Chicago. I'd still like to hear more about what the students were really like."

My sister's eyes got big and she stood up dramatically. "Oh my gosh, you should have seen them. From day one, they came in laughing and chewing gum and cracking jokes. They refused to sit down. They announced to me they didn't need no summer school. They hadn't failed any classes. They said they were big time high school seniors now, and furthermore, they knew more about Puerto Rican history than I would ever know."

I interrupted, "Yeah, I almost got cold feet at first. I thought, what have I gotten us into? The last three years I was teaching quiet respectful nursing students almost the same age in Mexico. And it was sure gonna be different from student teaching in Iowa."

Mom looked shocked, "Did you ever get them to settle down?"

Rachel said she did it by fitting in short history lessons while working most days with Carlos. His art classes transformed the drab yellow walls of the church basement into a brilliant colored mural of Puerto Rican flags and people with brown, black, and white faces working and celebrating together. "Puerto Rican Pride" in big red letters formed the centerpiece, in case anyone missed the point. Superimposed on a large map of the Puerto Rican island were three groups of people yelling at each other, one saying "Independence now"; another saying, "Statehood now"; and the third saying "Status quo." Rachel explained that this is an ongoing controversy in Puerto Rico.

Mom persevered in her questioning, "And you, Beverly, how did you win the students over?"

I said, "They started out being belligerent with me, too. They confronted me with, 'We ain't gonna take no tests or write no papers. We ain't gonna read no books either!' "

"I answered them, 'Well, that's good, because there is no text-book for this course.' I raised my arms toward the windows and said dramatically 'The city is our textbook.'"

I confessed to my parents that I learned about Chicago government keeping one week ahead of the students by studying official city-printed literature and newspapers and what I could remember from government class in high school. My main teaching technique was taking them on field trips to city hall in the Chicago Loop to visit the three branches of government. First we did the executive branch. To prepare, I asked them who the mayor was. That was easy. Mayor Richard Daley was the namesake of our summer program. Then I asked—when we find the executive offices, what matters can we bring up as citizens? The students were hesitant about going downtown to city hall, so I assured them that all public facilities are open to the public and we were the public. When we went, I could tell it made office workers and other people nervous to see our large group of Puerto Rican teenagers walking in city hall, even though the students were quiet and well behaved. I became accustomed to the silent curiosity we created by our presence everywhere we went. Then we spent several class periods after each field trip discussing what we learned.

The folks were very interested in government and politics, so I went on about the second field trip in which we visited the legislative branch, the aldermen's chambers. We found the office of the alderman representing Lincoln Park. We were told he was out of the city. One youth found his voice and asked the receptionist, "Why aren't there any Latino policemen?" The answer surprised all of us, "Hispanic men can apply to be policemen, but they have to be 18 to 35 years old and measure five foot seven inches tall or taller." We looked at each other. I was the only one in our whole group who was 5'7" and over eighteen, and I couldn't apply either, because I was female.

In subsequent classes, we clarified in class discussion that city laws are written by aldermen, and they can be challenged by the public and changed by aldermen in city council. Aldermen are elected by the people. That question about policemen helped the students gain motivation for learning more about the political system, because some of them said they had always dreamed of becoming policemen when they grew up. We shared the opinion that the height requirement unfairly prohibited most Latinos from becoming policemen in Chicago. They asked, who do they think are the policemen in Puerto Rico, in fact in Central American and South American countries? We had another rousing discussion about whether or not females could do police work as well as males.

Since our first field trip, students had been asking me to visit some stores on 'that great street State Street' so on the third field trip to the judicial branch, I relented. After visiting the judicial branch at City Hall, we walked over to State Street. Leaving the jewelry store, one young man came up to me and proudly showed me his "prize."

I stood up from the family dinner table and acted out my teacher part, also imitating the students' voices.

"I didn't see you buy that."

"How could I buy it? I don't have any money. It's okay though, because nobody saw me. They won't miss it. They have a lot more."

"Hey, kids, did anyone else pick up anything in the store?"

"Sure. We all did." Some showed me or their friends made them confess.

I shook my head. "Listen to me, and listen to me good. We're going back into that store and you are going to return those things."

They looked at me incredulously, so I reminded them that they were attending summer school in a church, and one of the Ten Commandments is 'Thou shalt not steal.' After a long moment, one girl broke the silence.

"Hey, home boys, we don't wanna get the church in no trouble. They're all right. None of these things cost that much. We can take our next paycheck and come back and buy 'em if we want 'em that bad." I was never so relieved when I heard a reluctant murmur of agreement.

I asked my parents to imagine the looks on the clerks' faces when the youth dumped their plunder on the counter and all simply said, "Sorry."

Mom affirmed me for transferring a deep-seated Christian value I learned in rural Iowa to the big city of Chicago—honesty.

Dad reminded us of a saying, " 'You can take the girl out of the country, but you can't take the country out of the girl.' " We all laughed. I had never heard the saying before, but I had many occasions to remember it in the next months and years.

After dessert, we women cleared the table, did dishes, and the folks decided to forego playing cards that evening as we usually did on our visits, because they wanted my sister and me to continue telling them the part of the summer job that was the scariest for us. Rachel said she hated going to Cabrini Greens. She almost didn't go the first time a school bus took all of us teachers and students to our sister Mayor Daley Summer Peace Corps program in the church near Cabrini Greens housing project. The purpose of the joint meeting was to hear a speaker on community organization. We sat down with our group of Latinos on one side of the church sanctuary. All the black students came in and sat together on the other side in a block. They had T-shirts with "Black is Beautiful" in big letters and sported Afro hair styles. We eyed each other suspiciously; however, our pastor-directors, Bruce and Maurice, talked to each other in a friendly manner before the meeting started.

I added I thought Bruce looked like Dick Van Dyke, but with horn-rimmed glasses. Maurice could have been a double for Richard Pryor.

Rachel continued the story that the leaders announced that our two groups would get together a few more times for speakers and field trips, because we needed to get to know each other as the summer progressed. The students from both racial ethnic blocks groaned in unison. Then everyone laughed. It broke the ice.

During the break, I told them about a scary thing that happened to me when I had asked to use their church pay phone (no cell phones back then). I put in my dime and then noticed the rotary dial was jammed with chewing gum, caked on solid. It wouldn't move. There were four or five black students and a teacher named Ivory standing nearby, so I asked if anyone had anything I could use to loosen up the phone dial. To my shock, every single student in the group whipped out a pocketknife and with eager faces, held them out, offering them to me. Ivory just watched with a deadpan look on his face; he didn't say or do anything.

Maurice came up to me after the meeting and kindly told me that Ivory told him how shocked I looked during the phone episode, but how fast I recovered my composure and chose one of the knives to free the phone dial. He asked me if I had ever thought of teaching in the city. He said public schools need teachers who care about the kids and aren't afraid of them demonstrating their survival skills.

I told him that I had my application in to teach in the Chicago Public School system. He nodded his approval, and then told me he had just finished his seminary internship, but he wanted to visit the African continent before he started serving in a church.

I admitted to my rapt family audience around the table that I liked it that he took an interest in me.

Rachel said accusingly, "You're blushing, Bev. I didn't know you had a crush on him."

"Rachel, you know that's not true. There's one thing I liked about the summer program. No flirting. Nobody 'hit on' anybody. We just all worked together for the kids and for the fun of it. Period."

Mom said. "Do you know what I keep thinking about? World Builders. Remember how we parents had the kids' meeting every month in church when you girls were growing up? Do you think that helped you to develop a good attitude about working with other races like you did this summer?"

"Yeah, it did, Mom," Rachel and I responded simultaneously.

"But our family having foreign student visitors here over Thanksgiving vacations helped us get to know real life people," I volunteered.

"I still have a lot to learn though, if I'm gonna stay and teach in Chicago, especially about blacks," Rachel said. "Bev, you tell 'em about our field trip to the DuSable Museum."

I told how the trip to the DuSable Museum of African American Culture and History in Washington Park on Chicago's south side was arranged by Ivory, the art and culture teacher with the other program. We went in a school bus. The DuSable Museum was housed temporarily in something like army barracks, actually a former Second World War Fifth Army vehicle storage building. In contrast, the paintings, art work, and sculptures inside were emotional and dramatic, depicting ardent and unfulfilled desires for freedom and equality from slavery days to present day sports figures. Our students were in silent awe as the guide led the way through the facility. Maya Angelou, the famous black poet laureate, had contributed sayings posted above the doors, seemingly directed at youth, encouraging them to take pride in their heritage.

"Rachel, you remember some of them, don't you?"

"Yes, my favorite was: 'How important it is for us to recognize and celebrate our heroes and she-roes.' Let me see. Another good one was: 'I believe that every person is born with talent.'—Maya Angelou."

"I think the kids' favorite went something like this: 'I've learned that you shouldn't go through life with a catcher's mitt on both hands; you need to be able to throw something back.' —Maya Angelou."

The folks were nodding their appreciation. I continued the story of the field trip. "I'll never forget the bus trip back home. We teachers were sitting near the front, talking to the driver, right, Rachel?" Rachel nodded.

The driver was telling us he was having trouble staying awake, since he didn't get enough sleep, driving being his second job. All of the sudden, there was a lot of noise behind us. I looked down the aisle just as one of the black youths was thrown down and another black youth pounced on him and was beating his face with his fists. I made a reflexive move toward them to try to get them to stop. Maurice grabbed my shoulder and held me back so I couldn't interfere. The driver kept driving.

Maurice warned me, "You'll just get yourself hurt or killed. The only time to try to stop a fight is before it starts. I don't know what this one is about. We'll just have to let them fight it out, and hope for the best." Before too long he did yell at them to stop. As I watched with horror, the aggressor stopped for a second. His friends quickly grabbed him and told him to cool it. The youth being pounded in the face put his hands to his bloody nose, got back up, sat down, and looked sadly at Maurice.

The bus driver came to a stop at a Cabrini Green bus stop. The black students stood up, including the victim, and filed silently off the bus. The black teachers got off two blocks further north at their church, muttering about talking with their kids about this incident the next day. The rest of us stayed on the bus for the last eight blocks. I was still in shock how violence had broken out in our Peace Corps group. I was concerned if no one cared about the victim, but I hoped I was wrong. I'd let myself be restrained and hadn't done anything to help him myself. But I learned something important—not to try to stop fights once they started in serious. There were definitely limits to what I could ever do to make things better for young people in Chicago.

Our father said he hoped we had steered clear of all the anti-war demonstrations in Chicago around the political convention. Rachel immediately told them she had nothing to do with the protests. I followed my intuition and my lack of courage, and somewhat dishonestly summed up my involvement by telling the folks I had paid some attention to them, but honestly decided against getting overly involved. We were here in Iowa after all, so we were missing the whole Democratic Convention week, which was also a week of protests against the Vietnam War. Rachel didn't contradict me.

Bedtime for me. I was tired from driving seven hours from Chicago to north central Iowa. I peeked out of my bedroom windows at the farm yard where I spent many hours of my childhood and youth doing chores after school. As I opened my suitcase, I saw a paper placed provocatively on the dresser. A closer look revealed it to be a mimeographed speech that was given at the 1968 American Farm Bureau Women's Annual Conference. I remembered Mom used to leave reading material for me from time to time on topics such as menstruation that she obviously didn't want to discuss openly with me. I scanned it to see why she wanted me to look at it and then sat down to read it.

"We can make it a first order of business to work today, and every day, to develop in ourselves, in our children, and in the people around us, an understanding and appreciation of this great big beautiful land that we call the United States. As a nation, we have become obsessed with talking about what's wrong with our country. We hear it in the halls of government. We hear it from each other. We hear it from the pulpit. Our children hear it in school. At home and abroad, America is being pictured as an ailing giant. Many people in the world are concluding that the United States is on the road to decline and downfall. Rioting in Washington, following the murder of Martin Luther King caused damage estimated to be in an amount almost nearing 24 million dollars. 'Communists are at the forefront in civil rights, antiwar and student demonstrations,' says Mr. Hoover. He tells us that in the last seven years, during which we lost 25,000 boys in Vietnam, while 67,000 people were murdered right here in our country. Now we cannot sit back and wait for things to right themselves, Mr. Hoover says a many-sided effort is necessary. If our country's youth really understood the greatness and the goodness of America, I do not think they would be doing the things that some of them are doing. I think it would go a long way toward eliminating the hippie, the juvenile delinquent, the pot smoker, the rioter, the drop out, the New Left, the unwed mother. And if our citizens really understood the greatness and the goodness of America, they would not permit our country to rush headlong into socialism and destroy the principles that made her great. They would pull back. And I believe they will."

I laid down to go to sleep, thinking about how hard it was in our family to confront differences in opinion and discuss them openly. We didn't want to 'disturb the peace.' Like this evening, I knew I had stopped myself from speaking up, when I could have said something about the war protests. I predicted I was going to have to change my fear of controversy and overcome this timidity when I became a high school teacher.

Rachel came up to get ready for bed after putting Markie to bed. I asked her, "Did you read that speech?"

"Yeah, and I noticed how you didn't tell Dad about Bobby Seale and those demonstrations you went to."

I shook my head. "We had such a nice night. I guess I didn't want to cause any dissension."

Rachel picked up the speech. "I wish I could talk to Mom about this speech and why she wants us to read it, but I don't know how to start. The speech seems so judgmental, and we're on the 'wrong side.' According to this speaker, any criticism of laws and policies in this great country of ours contributes to socialism and communism. I thought free speech contributed to democracy."

I mused, "Right on. The speaker is clearly against the types of people who protest the war, although she never mentions the war except to downplay the number of casualties of war compared to the casualties of violence here at home. I wonder if those numbers of casualties are really right. There's no awareness of why or what young people are protesting."

"I wonder what our folks really think about the Vietnam War. Aren't they proud of Erwin for being a conscientious objector or does his outspoken antiwar stance embarrass them with the neighbors?"

While my sister went to the bathroom to brush her teeth, I continued talking loudly enough so she and maybe my parents could hear me. "Well, I'm proud of him for standing up against the war and giving these years of his life for peace instead of war. Thank goodness for his alternative service with the Quakers (Society of Friends) teaching year-round vegetable farming using irrigation in a remote area of southern Laos. We'll have to ask the folks about how he's doing."

As I brushed my teeth and got ready for bed, I thought about how the Vietnam War was changing all of us kids' lives in our family even though we were not directly involved. I knew as I relished each new experience in the city, I was also an Iowa farm girl. I didn't think it was hurting me to give up some of my absolutist right or wrong thinking and become more open-minded. But how could I stay true to myself if I couldn't talk with my own mother about things we didn't agree on? To get to sleep, I took Dietrich Bonhoeffer's *The Cost of Discipleship* off a shelf. Written during the Second World War before he became a martyr, the book had always fascinated me and I randomly picked out a page on the topic of peace to re-read.

> 'Blessed are the peacemakers: for they shall be called the children of God.' The followers of Jesus have been called to peace. When he called them they found their peace, for he is their peace. But now they are told that they must not only *have* peace but *make* it. And to that end they renounce all violence and tumult. In the cause of Christ nothing is to be gained by such methods. His kingdom is one of peace, and the mutual greeting of his flock is a greeting of peace. His disciples keep the peace by choosing to endure suffering themselves rather than inflict it on others. They maintain fellowship where others would break it off. They renounce all self-assertion, and quietly suffer in the face of hatred and wrong. In so doing they overcome evil with good, and establish the peace of God in the midst of a world of war and hate. (Bonhoeffer, Dietrich, *The Cost of Discipleship*. New York: SCM Press, 1959; Simon & Schuster 1995, pp. 112-113).

At the bottom of a page I had taken some notes. I asked: what is peace? Here is what it is not: not safety, not security, not self-protection, not selfish purposes. Here is what it is: daring, faith, trust, the greater good. Yes, I had come to like Bonhoeffer, because he was a young adult like me when he was dealing with war and peace with so much courage, I knew I would never understand him, but I found his writings compelling and I admired him.

That night I had a dream that I was in a line of Peace Corps workers carrying baskets of food and soccer balls and toys for children into one of the villages of Vietnam where the enemy had taken refuge. I imagined the women and children rushing toward us to see what we brought and in turn inviting us to a feast of local foods.

CHAPTER 3
Our End-Of-Summer Party

At the end-of-summer meeting, the teachers from the other Mayor Daley's Peace Corps program by Cabrini Greens joined us in the Armitage Methodist Church basement. Carlos and several students were finishing painting the back hallway of the church, so he slipped in and out of the meeting. The rest of us pulled chairs together for an informal session with our directors. After Bruce and Maurice passed out the final paychecks, Maurice stopped and cleared his throat.

"There is something important we all need to recognize. We can be very proud of what happened this summer—in fact, the biggest accomplishment is that three distinct ethnic groups worked voluntarily together for a common cause. I have never seen this kind of collaboration until this summer."

Bruce then spoke with passion, almost as though he were delivering a sermon. "I'm sure the students came to share our vision—the idea that they have some power to change themselves and change things in their community. You teachers have done a great job equipping them to continue learning and caring. I cannot overemphasize that. Does anyone have anything else to bring up?"

My sister Rachel surprised everyone, including me. "Aren't we gonna have a farewell party? All of us together?"

Maurice spoke up first, "Well, I would really like that, but I'll be leaving in a week and a half for my long-awaited trip to Ethiopia. If we could put off the party until I get back, I could tell you all about my trip."

Bob Ratsos, the summer cook in the Armitage program, said, "No man, we can't wait. Most of us will be off to our own future lives by then. You know we have places to go and things to do and people to see." Everyone laughed. He continued, "No seriously, if we are going to do it, we need to do it right away."

Frank Tatum, a teacher in the sister program, asked, "Where will the party be? A church ain't no place for a real party." He looked around the group. "Someone's gotta have a pad big enough for a party."

"We do!" Rachel waved her hand like one of the students. "My sister and I and our roommate live in an apartment right behind Wrigley Field, corner of Waveland and Sheffield." I heard a murmur of interest from the group.

The glaring exception was Ivory. "I ain't goin' to no honky's crib. No way." Ivory stiffened up and shook his head, emphasizing his no. "Maybe black and white mixed this summer, but this summer program ain't real life. Black and white don't mix that much, like at parties. *Shi-i-it no!*"

Rachel smiled, "That's okay. You don't have to come, Ivory, but you'll miss out, because we're gonna take everyone up to the roof of the building and show you where people can watch the Chicago Cubs' games for free."

Ivory seemed to back off with a little smile, and his tone changed. "For real? Right on, li'l sister."

Carlos popped in after checking on the painting squad, "Cool. If there's gonna be a party, what are we gonna have to eat?" Suddenly the whole focus changed.

"Oh, yeah," Frank said. "My partying depends on what we're gonna eat."

Rachel looked at me. "What'll it be, Bev?"

Not prepared for making a menu commitment, I suggested tentatively, "Submarine sandwiches?"

Bob groaned, "That's boring. How's about something more exciting?"

"Okay, mister cooking expert," I said. "How's about you help us figure this out?"

"I just thought of something better. What about sloppy-Joes?"

"What're sloppy-Joes?"

"You know. Brown some ground beef, add tomato sauce, Worcestershire sauce, spices, and serve on a hamburger bun." All summer Bob loved to be asked how he made something we liked.

"That sounds like something we call "made-rites" in Iowa."

"I never heard of made-rights, but that's cool. I can get to the party early and make sloppy-Joes. They're easy."

"Thanks, Bob, I'll let you know. We need to talk to our roommate first. What'll we do about drinks? We always have soda pop and lemonade on hand. Could the rest be BYOB (bring your own booze)? Let's not have anything harder than beer though. Agreed?"

"What about Ripple?" asked Frank. "I'll bring some to share. What'd'ya say?"

"Sure, if you bring 'em."

Rachel said, "One last thing: MUSIC!"

Ivory piped in, "Yeah, y'all probably only got records like they play on American Bandstand. Rock 'n roll. White people love rock 'n roll. Now, Chuck Berry, he's the man who invented rock 'n roll, and I think he's the best ever. He never got invited to no American Bandstand. He says he's too black."

I had enough of Ivory's veiled insults. I decided to stand up to him. "Why let that stop you? You're invited to the party. Why don't you bring some Chuck Berry rock and roll singles?"

He ignored my question. "So tell the truth, Bev, do you have any soul music records at your house?"

I thought quickly. "I have one—*Keeping On Keeping On*, by Aretha Franklin. And you know what? It's a good one to listen to when people are bugging you unfairly."

"You white folks surprise me sometimes."

Carlos piped in. "Salsa is Latin soul music! I'll bring salsa."

Another teacher called out, "Jazz! I got a great jazz collection. I'll bring Ramsey Lewis' *The In Crowd*. You'll love that one."

Rachel's voice came back in above the male voices. "How about a week from tomorrow? Saturday at seven o'clock." Everyone voiced approval. Rachel told Maurice she wished he could be there.

Maurice answered, "Oh, I'll be there. I won't be leaving for Ethiopia until the week after that. I wouldn't miss this party for anything."

I was aware that Pastor Bruce hadn't said anything. "What about you, Bruce? You've been quiet. Is there any chance we can count on you coming?"

"I've been enjoying listening. You did some good problem solving, folks, but I'm really sorry. I can't attend. I have a lot of early Sunday morning commitments in the church. You know, summer's over. Gotta get back to business as usual, but you go ahead—have fun. You have my blessing."

The group got up and mingled, continuing to talk about music and bringing favorite records. The idea of sharing music appealed to everyone. Others variously told me they would bring pop (soft drinks) and wine coolers. The happy prospects of this get-together ended our official summer program on a high note.

Rachel fell in with Ivory as he was walking out. "Ivory, if you change your mind about coming, we'd love to have you."

Ivory mumbled something like, "Don't count on it."

⁂

When we got back to the apartment, my sister Rachel, my roommate Janice, and I got our heads together about the food for the party. Janice had her secretary clothes on and with her glasses and smoothly combed brown hair, she looked very business-like. She had a job as a secretary at McCormick Theological Seminary in Lincoln Park. She said she was pleased that she would finally meet the co-workers we had been talking about all summer.

I got to know Janice when I first moved to Chicago. She was the only person I ever met in Chicago that sprinkled sugar on sliced tomatoes in a salad like I did. We decided it had to be the Pennsylvania Dutch influence, because she was from Pennsylvania. My grandmother's parents were from Pennsylvania and Grandma still spoke Pennsylvania Dutch with her sisters. We decided that food customs are passed down through the women, the cooks of the family. Janice and I found we had a lot of interests in common in addition to food and decided to room together to share housing expenses.

"We have a problem," said Rachel, "because we're talking about a lot of different tastes—Puerto Ricans, blacks, and whites—all guys!"

"Whew, that's a problem." Janice ran her fingers through her hair like she always does when she's thinking hard and then patted it back in place. "What would be something everyone likes that would fill 'em up?"

I mimicked the guys, "What's there to eat? That's all we care about. What's to eat?"

Rachel said, "That is mostly what they cared about, Janice."

A sudden inspiration came to me, "How about an early Thanksgiving dinner? Everyone celebrates Thanksgiving. We could use the frozen turkey we just brought back from Iowa."

"Yes!" Rachel and Janice agreed instantly

I realized this was some serious cooking to make turkey and dressing and accompaniments for a group of all guys. "I have an idea. Let's call Bob Ratsos. He's the one who cooked all summer for the program. Everyone really liked his cooking. They kept telling him he was so good he should open his own restaurant."

"Is he coming?"

"He volunteered to come early and make sloppy-Joes for the party if we wanted them. They are so sloppy though. I'll tell him what we're deciding on."

"He could come up with the recipes even if he doesn't know 'em already."

"I'll call him and see if he can do it," I offered.

"You know? This is like a real Thanksgiving dinner, isn't it?" Rachel clapped her hands.

Janice said with a smile, "Yeah. Thank God you two got through the summer program alive and in one piece."

Seven o'clock came and went. No one was on time to the party. Bob Ratsos had all the food ready in the kitchen and it smelled delectable. I stood looking out of the front windows at the street below, wondering if anyone was going to come after all. Cars whizzed by. People were walking their dogs while it was still light. The "bag lady" as we called her sat on the curb on the other side of the street, sorting out her day's acquisitions. There were still parking places on the street because there was no Cubs home game that Saturday, thank goodness. Rachel picked up the phone and dialed a phone number. No answer.

"What's going on?" Rachel sounded impatient, "I suppose they're on their way. I can't believe everyone is so late."

"Did you ever think that maybe no one's coming?"

"Wouldn't that be a bummer?"

"Or—maybe they're all on their way. Chicago time isn't Iowa time ... or Pennsylvania time."

"Y'know, Bev, you're right. Most parties don't even start until nine o'clock or ten. I am so glad Mamita and Papito said they would be more than happy to babysit Markie overnight. And Markie just loves it when Mamita talks baby talk with him in Spanish. Wouldn't it be great if he could grow up knowing two languages?"

"I'm glad Markie is so happy since you brought him here after staying with his grandparents in Iowa all summer. He's such a happy little boy."

Just then I saw a two-tone blue '60 Chevy slowly drive past the apartment building and make a U-turn at the corner. It took a parking place across the street in front of the bag lady.

"Rachel! Come here and look whose coming to dinner!" Rachel fairly flew to the window. Her eyes and her mouth opened wide.

"Ivory! I can't believe it! He's the last one I thought would come, and here he is first!"

We opened the door of the apartment and watched as Ivory, Frank, and three other guys who I assumed were friends of theirs stomped solemnly up the stairs.

"Come on in!" Rachel and I were both smiling from ear to ear.

Ivory mumbled, "Hi, Rachel, Bev, these brothers are friends of ours; they hang out with us at the church." He spoke too fast for me to catch their names.

"Welcome. We're glad you came." I was surprised how tall Ivory and his friends were, and he seemed to be genuinely happy in the presence of his friends.

"Brought some records," said Ivory. "I even found some songs on the theme!"

"What theme is that?"

"Come on, Bev. What'd'ya think? Peace! Isn't that what we were all doing this summer? Working for Mayor Daley's Peace Corps program?" As he spoke, he held up his hand with the peace sign. I responded with the peace sign.

"Right on! I can hardly wait to hear the songs you chose. Here's our record player."

"Don't you have a turntable so we can play one after the other?"

"Nope. Sorry. This is just a plain, old record player, but it plays 33s and 45s. Where's that adapter? Here it is." (A 33 is a large record that turns 33 1/3 revolutions per minute on a turntable. It is also called a long-play record and has some twenty songs on one side. A 45 is a smaller record with a larger hole in the center which turns 45 revolutions per minute on the turntable. It is also called a single and has one hit song on one side and another song on the back side.)

"Well, dudes," Ivory motioned to his friends, "let's just have a seat and wait for Carlos and his buddies. Y'all know about Latin time, right? Seven o'clock means nine o'clock or whenever you can get there."

We all laughed. I couldn't believe what they did next. They sat in the chairs, side by side, and got completely quiet, putting on poker faces, like people do on public transportation. To me, it was embarrassing. I tried to fill the silence, "Ratsos is in the kitchen, y'know. Do ya want something to eat now?"

"Naw," said Ivory. "We'll just wait for the party to begin."

I took my station at the front window. Rachel went out to the kitchen. She and Janice started bringing in bottles of Coca Cola and Pepsi Cola, also an ice bucket and paper cups. Pure silence. I realized they must be as nervous as I was—me, because I didn't know if anyone else would show up—them, because they probably didn't know how to act around white people. Me again, because I didn't know what else to do to make them feel welcome.

All of the sudden, I saw two motorcycles and two cars with loud mufflers come tearing down the street, all make the U turn, and go a little slower in front of our apartment building. They then went their separate ways to different parking places. They emerged from the cars, coalesced as a group, rang the doorbell and I heard them climbing the stairs, two or three at a time, talking loudly in the usual mixture of Spanish and English.

As I went to the door, Ivory and his group jumped up and everyone greeted each other with high fives and *que pasa*? (What's happening?) "What's going down?"

"Hey, check out them 'fros!" Frank said.

Sure enough, most of the Puerto Ricans were sporting afro hair styles of all colors ranging from light brown to black, all lengths from short to long. They must have done them up especially for the party, because I didn't remember seeing any in the summer. Everyone was dressed like they did all summer, in blue jeans, jean cut offs (literally), khakis, plain color tee-shirts. Carlos brought some dance music records—*merengue* and *salsa*. He spotted the record player, put a 45 on, and turned up the volume. The noise level in the living room went up many decibels and stayed there for the next hour or so.

Bob, Rachel, and I brought out the food, much to everyone's approval. Voracious appetites kicked into gear. At one point I counted fifteen people, eleven guys and my sister and me. Janice stayed out in the kitchen most of the time helping Bob get the food ready.

"What happened to Maurice?" I asked Ivory. "Didn't he say he was gonna come?"

"Yeah, but he told me he'd be late. We should begin without him, but save him some food," he said with a smile. Just then the doorbell rang. Rachel opened the door and there stood Maurice, looking all handsome in a black three-piece suit, white shirt and narrow black and white striped necktie.

"I apologize for being late to the party, but I just gave the funeral of another brother. He was stabbed to death in a fight over a girl. It's such a loss."

"Well, come eat some of Ratsos' cooking for one last time," Rachel took his arm and led him to the food table. "That'll make you feel better."

Carlos bowed down giving a mock introduction of Maurice to his companions, "Hey, 'mano, you know what we say? *Buenas tardes*! It's a play on words. *Buenas tardes* means good afternoon. It also means good and late!"

Everyone laughed including Maurice. He bowed equally low and said, "How do you say: Better late than never?"

"*Mejor que vengas tarde que nunca vengas,*" Carlos translated with a big smile.

Everyone laughed heartily and clapped. Without missing a beat, I said loudly, "That is a perfect lead-in to the game I wanted us to play. It's a version of the TV show 'This is your life.' We just spent two months of our lives working with each other this summer. We might never see each other again. I'd like us all to share what we plan to do in the next year." I continued, "We'll get Maurice to tell us about his plans to travel to Ethiopia, but we'll allow him to eat first. He can be second. Who wants to go first?"

"Me!" Carlos jumped up. "I'm going to Puerto Rico as soon as I get airplane tickets. This past summer, me working with the kids painting those murals on the church basement walls reminded me of all the buildings with murals in Puerto Rico, and I got psyched up to go and take part in the politics there. They're going to have a referendum on the status of Puerto Rico. I'm going to work for the independence movement, man! I think the people need to be free."

Someone asked, "Aren't they free now?"

"No, 'mano. Puerto Rico is a territory under the control of the US. They have some of the benefits of citizenship, but they got no vote in national elections. There's a three-way split back home. One group wants independence, one wants the status quo, and there's another movement to make Puerto Rico the 51st state. You know, how Alaska and Hawaii became the 49th and 50th states back in 1959."

"That's cool, man. Where you gonna shack up?"

"I'll be staying with an aunt and uncle. It'll be a little dicey, 'cause I'll be promoting independence. They're teachers and they are paying Medicare taxes and Social Security taxes and will receive those benefits at retirement. They think that's enough, even though they can't vote in national elections. But they said they respect my convictions. I hope so."

Ivory rifled through his records and found one, "Here is a perfect background song for you, Carlos. 'Everybody everywhere just wanna be free!' " The lyrics were blasting out and music filled the room.

Carlos continued, "Y'know, Reverend Johnson—Bruce, that is—changed my life. He made me realize that all people can determine their own lives, not just the well-to-do, not just the politicos, not even the church. Everyone has vested interests. I want to help my people stand up proud and know they have choices in this world. I'll help them get over their fear of rocking the boat. Change is okay." We all continued listening, everyone lost in his or her own thoughts, until the song ended—"people everywhere just wanna be free."

Maurice set his plate down. "Carlos, you just summarized the whole summer program. That was a great statement. Thank you, bro. Now I have a simple question for you. I don't need a passport to take a vacation in Puerto Rico, do I?"

"You're right. You don't need a passport," answered Carlos, "'cause Puerto Rico's actually an E.L.A.—*Estado Libre Asociado* (a Free-Associated Commonwealth.) We're all American citizens. Everyone can travel back and forth freely. Going from Chicago to Puerto Rico is just like going from Chicago to California."

Maurice said, "But I need a passport where I'm going—Ethiopia! I'll bet y'all didn't know Ethiopia is such an old country, it's actually in the Bible?"

"Wow."

"Ethiopia is on the African continent." Maurice continued, "My ancestors came from Africa in slavery. I have always longed to go to Africa. Everyone here is here because our ancestors came from some other country overseas somewhere. For me, now's the time to learn about my African roots while I'm young and don't have anything or anyone to tie me down. I'm going to visit a church mission project, a little like President Kennedy's Peace Corps."

"What do they do there?"

"High school. The thing is that there is practically no education for girls in Ethiopia, in any Muslim country for that matter. Only boys go to public schools, which are really religious schools. The school I am going to is a Christian church-run school. They get a lot of flak for giving women and girls an education."

"That sucks."

"I don't think there will be peace anywhere in the world until women and men can sit down at the table together and treat each other equally and with respect. Women are just naturally more peace-loving. We saw that in our program all summer—who were the ones fighting all the time? Who tried to solve problems peacefully? You know as well as I do."

"I wish I could do something like you're gonna do," someone said. "But I need a job. You don't get paid for mission work, do you?"

"The missionaries make enough to live on: one thousand five hundred dollars for one year. Out of that they have to pay travel and fifteen a month for room and board. Me, I'm not gonna be paid. I'm gonna do volunteer work for a few months teaching English, Bible study, and history. It's enough I'll be surrounded by all girls and women. I'll probably feel like I died and went to heaven."

Ivory put on another record, "What the world needs now is love, sweet love." Everyone laughed and hooted. While they were all talking at once, Rachel slipped out and brought back the college graduation picture of our brother, which she showed around the group.

"This is my brother, Erwin. He's overseas right now. You know where?"

"Tell us, li'l sister," said Ivory.

"Well, Erwin refused to go to war. So the draft board made him a conscientious objector. He's in Laos now, right over there next to Vietnam. He's out in the countryside teaching year-round irrigation farming. He's been there more than two years."

"I didn't know there was any way to get out of going to war without having something wrong with you. Isn't that why some guys are moving to Canada? Mohammed Ali's in jail because he refused to be conscripted," Ivory said as he put on the record. *Give peace a chance.* "What if they started a war and no one went? That would be a good one."

"Right on!" Bob came out from the kitchen with some new information, "I know two of us who got drafted but we ain't going, right, Ivory?" He whipped out an official-looking piece of paper and proudly showed it around the group. "This is a 2-F classification. It means they don't want me in the Army. I can't hear outta one ear. But Ivory's 2-F beats them all. Tell 'em, man!"

"I got flat feet." Everyone laughed.

"Well, lucky you. Those things don't sound so bad. What are you two going to do with all your freedom next year?"

Bob said, "This next year I get prepared for my dream job. I wanna open my own restaurant. I have a really different idea. I want to make it ultramodern with slideshows projected on the walls of contemporary musicians, movie stars, and sports heroes. I'll play all kinds of popular music. I want to make the food so mostly young people, singles, will come—like in their 20s and maybe 30s. Chicago hot dogs, sloppy-Joes, pizza with twenty choices for different toppings. Yeah, I want to make it a fun place to be. And here's the really important part. It won't just be for whites or blacks or Latinos. I want everyone to come—all races and all nationalities of people."

Ivory put on another record and we listened to the words, "Come on, people now; smile on me, brother; everybody get together; try to love one another right now."

Ivory looked over at Bob. "Hey, Bob, I would go eat there if I could find it and afford it."

"Oh, you'll be able to find it. I'm going to find a place in Lincoln Park or Lakeview and I'm gonna call it Ratsos. We'll have affordable menu items, trust me." I'm aiming at two or three years from now. Next year I need to work in some restaurant in the Lettuce-Entertain-You chain to get experience and save money. And I wanna take some courses in culinary arts, business, and management. My dad is going to help me. Okay, Ivory, it's your turn. What d'you plan on doing?"

"I've already made a connection with the senior pastor in the church where we worked this summer. We're going to keep the summer program going as an after school program. And we're going to open it up to younger boys. My homeboys here and me are gonna work it. We're going to turn fourth, fifth, and sixth graders on to something besides selling drugs and gang-banging. And check this out! The church fathers said we can paint the walls of the basement. We gonna beat you out, Carlos. We gonna put your walls to shame!"

"Impossible! But you might come in a close second. Bruce is gonna let them Young Lords start a day care center in the church basement on Armitage. Little kids writing on our walls? They'll never be the same, man."

"Yeah, something might go wrong for us, too. The city has slated our church and the whole area around us to be torn down for urban renewal. We don't know when, right, Maurice?"

"Unfortunately we don't know if the church'll have to move away from Cabrini Greens. They say they're even going to tear down all those Cabrini Greens projects sometime in the future."

"Good luck, Ivory. I hope you keep it going as long as you can," I said. "That leaves Rachel and me. You go first, sis."

"Bev and I both got teaching jobs here in Chicago. I just found out I'm gonna be at Carpenter Elementary School."

"And I just found out I'm gonna be at Waller High School."

"I can't believe it!" said Carlos. "Bev, you're going to have the same kids we had in the summer program. That's going to be a trip."

"Yeah, won't they be surprised!"

Maurice stood up and came over to Rachel and me, putting his arms around our shoulders, "That is very happy news for me.

I always thought you two were called to teach. Government and history can be the most boring subjects of all, but you two brought them alive, applied everything to the lives of the kids, and got them actively involved in their own learning. Lucky the schools that are getting you two as teachers!"

Maurice continued, "While I still have the floor, I have something else really important to say to all of you. I am so proud you are all still committed to making Chicago a better place to live. I can't tell you in words how happy you make me feel. You give me hope. We all know this very minute there are angry people planning more violent demonstrations against the Vietnam War. They say they want to 'bring the war home.' There are people planning riots for the anniversary of Doctor Martin Luther King's assassination instead of remembering he was a man of peace."

Maurice sighed. "You could have gone that route, but no, you're choosing to be the peacemakers of tomorrow. I just have to remind you that Jesus said, 'Blessed are the peacemakers for they will be called the children of God.' God bless each one of you. Peace! Paz! Shalom!"

The party ended with lots of hugs and high-fives. No one even remembered the roof tour idea. After everyone left, Rachel, Janice, and I straightened up the living room and cleaned the kitchen in silence, each lost in our own thoughts. I felt the best thing about the party was the joy of telling our plans for the future. We teachers were all so different, yet we were united in wanting to work for a better world. The music topped it off. I had no idea there were so many popular songs about longing for peace and racial harmony. I was amazed by the seemingly genuine transformation in Ivory. He actually called Rachel, "little sister."

I was happy she didn't let his anti-white talk stop her from letting him know he was welcome at the party and it was his decision to come or not to come. Her courage gained his respect. The party was truly a perfect ending for a summer that had changed all of our lives for the better. I knew I was changing in ways that cannot be learned in books, only gained through the experience of living, working, and caring about people around me.

CHAPTER 4

Chicago Public School Newbie

LABOR DAY, 1968

I spent Labor Day nervously imagining how my first day of teaching at Waller High School would play out. Looking over the students' names on my classroom lists and my division (home room) list I was given at orientation, I found no familiar names. I felt a mixture of relief and disappointment, because I was fond of the teenagers in Mayor Daley's Peace Corps summer school program, but I didn't want to play favorites on my new job. The school was located just three blocks from the Armitage Avenue church.

The next day I reported to work early and went to Room 203, my assigned classroom. The bulletin boards were decorated for Textiles and Clothing, the classes held in that room.

7:50 A.M. The first passing bell rang and a wave of noisy students poured into the school building. I stood in the hallway outside my classroom as teachers were supposed to do during passing periods. The first students I saw were running straight toward my classroom, and I could hear them all the way down the hall laughing and talking about "seeing Beverly first" before going to classes. It was a happy homecoming, with hugs and greetings, even though we had been working together just two weeks earlier.

All of a sudden it occurred to me that they were calling me Beverly, my summer school name. It didn't seem proper for a teacher to be called by her first name in a public school. I had to think fast and said, "Hey, guys, you're gonna have to call me Miss Johnson here in the school."

"A-a-a-aw no, that's not fair," they complained loudly.

"I'll never remember," one said, "all summer you were Beverly to us."

I scratched my head. "Okay, let's compromise. How about if you call me Miss Beverly? And that's a special privilege for summer school kids only. I won't let anyone else call me Miss Beverly."

"Aw, okay. We gotta go. See ya!" Off they went to their first period classes. They would not have me for their teacher, thank goodness, but I knew I was still in their hearts. And that meant a lot to me. Most of them were seniors, which made them special in a school system where half of the students dropped out by the time of graduation.

The next wave of students walking down the hallway consisted of very young-looking ninth graders searching for the room to which they were assigned for division. The students seemed to be about one-third blacks, one-third whites/Anglos/Asians, and one-third Hispanics. They were wide-eyed, eager, smiling, and much quieter than the summer school upperclassmen and women I had just encountered moments earlier.

8:00 A.M. The tardy bell rang. We had long division—twenty minutes to call roll, record attendance, listen to announcements over the intercom, and answer students' questions about the day's schedule. I realized at once that I was going to have to memorize these thirty-five names right away or I wouldn't have time for anything other than taking attendance.

By the time my classes came and went that day, I had about 140 names to memorize. I gave myself one week to learn them all. I suspected that the students would catch on quickly if I couldn't call them by name. I could imagine them taking advantage of that situation.

I knew that first day that one of my major challenges during my first year of teaching would be to try to understand and relate to urban black students. I had done my student teaching with white students in an Iowa town and I had taught Hispanic students in Mexico and again last summer, but I had never worked with African American students before. The other major challenge would be to learn how to maintain classroom discipline with all these city kids, while at the same time teaching the curriculum. Discipline and relationships might be contradictory; time would tell.

A black student named Terrence stayed after division and said, "Miss Johnson, you told us to come and talk to you if we have any school concerns. You said you will be our division teacher all through high school, and you want us to graduate in four years. Miss Johnson, you wait and see," he said pointing dramatically to himself, "I'm gonna pass all my classes, and I'll be here in your division all four years. I wonder if anyone else'll do the same." He laughed and he raised his right hand to give me my first "high five" ever, in recognition of his promise to me and his commitment to his high school education. Four years later, he reminded me that he kept his promise. He was right. He was the only one of the original thirty-five ninth graders still in my division to graduate with the class of 1972.

From time to time, Terrence took me up on my offer to be of help. My division room got changed to Room 207, the Foods and Nutrition classroom, with a clothes washer and dryer in one corner. He brought his gym clothes and towel occasionally to wash and dry. He explained something about having difficulty doing laundry at home. Since he did the work himself, I decided not to complain when I found his clothes in the dryer. He always came back for them.

I learned from him that it only took a little personal attention to develop a bond with a student. I began to believe that when I showed I cared a little, it made a big difference. I could see it became much more likely the student would succeed if some adult believed in him or her. The ratio of students to teachers was very high compared to my student teaching high school, but I took that as another challenge to get to know all my students as individuals.

There were three home economics teachers in the department, including me. Both of the others had taught for many years, and they served as mentors for me. They were not overbearing. On the contrary, they seemed to be tickled when I told them the things I wanted to do. I got to know them and several other teachers better, when they invited me to join their teachers' bowling group.

I had three Clothing classes which met in three single periods of forty minutes and two laboratory classes, which were double periods, making a total of seven periods of class time per week. The students were to learn to sew and actually construct garments for themselves, as well as learn about fabrics and grooming. I soon learned the conditions that made it difficult to teach an effective Textiles and Clothing program in the inner city. For one, the students in the classes were almost all below poverty level. Most had somewhere between very little and no money to buy their sewing equipment, fabric, and pattern for their sewing projects. Another difficulty was the safety issue. Shears or a big needle could jab its holder in the face or it could be used like a knife for threatening another student. I decided to prevent such behavior by empha- sizing the correct way to hold and carry a shears, actually like my mother had taught me—always with the points down. None of the students had the foggiest idea how to manipulate a sewing machine. Yet they were highly motivated to learn how to sew, so they could have a new blouse and pair of slacks or skirt. Since they wanted the immediate gratification of a new outfit, I needed somehow to encourage more patience and persistence. A bright idea occurred to me one day. A spring fashion show with students in all the Clothing classes would offer tangible long-term gratification. Perhaps we could use the school auditorium. I floated the idea in the classes and got positive feedback.

Foods and Nutrition was my other class. It was also a seven-period class and presented its own challenges. A big surprise to me was how few students had ever sat down at a table with a place setting in front of them to eat a family-style meal. The safety issue involved scissors and knives in the kitchen units, where students would work in groups of four. Those tools held the same temptations as the shears and needles in the clothing classroom.

I asked the students why they signed up for Foods and Nutrition. I wanted to address their motivations. Their answers surprised me. They told me how many new restaurants were opening up on the near north side of Chicago, and they hoped to get a job as a waitress or a cook one day. I asked permission to set aside the basic food preparation curriculum and start with a one semester Waiter and Waitress Training Course. The second semester I planned to teach basic restaurant cooks' helper techniques, including use of kitchen tools, safety, sanitation, nutrition, and some basic food preparation skills from the regular curriculum. Of course, it was approved by my supportive department chair.

To establish classroom discipline, I spent one whole week of classes on goals and motivation—developing a vision of skills and outcomes the students could expect in that class. I told them

I knew we could accomplish the classroom goals, and I hoped they believed they could, too. It occurred to me to say that now they knew what I would do for them as their teacher. The second week I went over their part—what they had to do, how they had to cooperate. I went over discipline rules, safety rules, and the correct vocabulary for work tools. The third week I finally started into the curriculum, but I stopped everything whenever there was any disrespectful misbehavior or incorrect classroom language such as swearing or angry outbursts. I dealt with problems immediately. Before long, the students started correcting each other, so classroom work didn't have to come to a halt for that day. Although I had not planned it that way ahead of time, it worked very well. And I learned an important lesson about running a high school classroom. It is an unwritten contract between a teacher and students. A teacher cannot teach anything without the cooperation of the students. In other words, the students had to buy into what I was teaching before they gave me "permission" to teach them.

One Saturday morning the apartment doorbell rang while my roommates and I were sitting in the front room reading the newspaper. Peering through the peephole, seeing a white middle-aged man wearing a dress suit and hat, holding up a badge, we opened the three locks on the door. He showed us his badge and said, "Federal Bureau of Investigation. I'm looking for Beverly Johnson. I would like to ask her a few questions."

"I'm Beverly. Won't you come in?" I had implicit trust in policemen and law officials, yet I wondered what in the world this was about. I invited him into the front room. "Please sit down. This is my roommate, Janice, and sister, Rachel. How can I help you?"

"I just have a few questions for you about your activities on August 28."

I must have looked puzzled because he continued by explaining, "That was during the Democratic Convention. But ladies, before we get started, maybe I could have some coffee? Do you happen to have any?"

"Oh yes, of course," offered Janice. "I'll go get us all some. I'll have to make it though. It'll only take a minute." She left, seemingly glad to get away from the questioner.

The agent opened a notebook and asked me if I drove a 1957 black and white Ford out to the airport last August 28. Rachel said accusingly, "See, Bev? I told you that you should never have done that. I was afraid you were gonna get into trouble."

"Don't worry. You're not in trouble, Beverly. We know you left the city the next day, before the Democratic Convention started. Oh, by the way, Rachel, did I mention I wanted cream with my coffee?"

"We don't have any cream. How about milk?" Rachel asked. He nodded. Rachel got up and went out to the kitchen.

As soon as she left, he again thought of something else, "Oh, I forgot to tell the girls that I need a little sugar boost in the morning. Could you bring some sugar, too?"

"Sure, okay, I'll get some sugar," I said affably. I felt a little strange leaving him alone in the front room, but I couldn't yell out his request, because I knew they couldn't hear back in the kitchen from the front room. All yelling would do was wake up little Markie. The layout of the apartment was a long rectangle, the front room facing Sheffield Avenue, next an arched opening into the living room, then a wall separating the three bedrooms and one bathroom in a row with doorways facing the hallway, and finally a dining room and kitchen in the back with an outer door which opened to a wooden porch and staircase ending in the back alley. So I walked down the long hallway leading to the kitchen in the back of the apartment and helped my roommates put together the breakfast coffee tray.

When we returned to the living room, the FBI agent had a scrapbook laid out on a table open to pages containing photographs. After everyone got their cup of coffee and he doctored his with milk and sugar, he asked me if I could identify any of the men as the ones who rode with me in my car that day in August. He flipped the pages and gave me a chance to study the pictures. All were black men. I stopped him after a few pages and asked, "How did you know when I left the city?"

"The FBI has its ways."

I could see he wasn't going to say any more. I continued to flip the pages, looking at pictures. Finally, I recognized one as Bobby Seale. The agent nodded and closed the book. Then he asked questions about the circumstances surrounding my drive to the airport and what Bobby Seale said in the car about his Chicago plans. I tried to answer as honestly as I could. He asked for the names of my companion in the car, any other drivers, the teachers in the summer program, and the peace protesters from Ohio. I cooperated as much as I was able—naming four or five names.

Then he said, "I wonder if you have their phone numbers."

I shook my head. "I don't have any phone numbers. Actually never did. We never needed to call anybody. We saw each other at work every day. I could give you the church phone number."

"No, that's not necessary. We have it. Do you think you could inquire further and get me phone numbers or addresses of the people you dealt with this past summer?"

"I really don't know—unless I had some time to try calling a few people who might have their numbers."

"Well, I would really appreciate that. How long would you need—a couple of weeks?"

"I suppose so. I'll try."

Then he left, strangely enough leaving over half the cup of coffee he said he wanted so badly. (snooping)?

*

I needed to work on lesson plans that day like I did every Saturday. Rachel and Janice were both going out somewhere, so I said I would stay home and watch Markie. I was feeling sad anyway, because John, my only love interest at the time, was turning out to be a two-timer. He was going to be busy that Saturday night, so I decided to have another cup of coffee and pour out my feelings in my journal, which I had kept over all the years ever since it was required by a high school English teacher. I only wrote in it when I was inspired or deeply concerned about someone or something. My last writing entry was March eleventh when I was still living in my Prairie Shores apartment right beside Michael Reese Hospital, where I was working at the time. I thought, *Wow, a lot has happened since that day when John asked me if we were going to get married when he turned thirty years old.* I had said yes, and claimed in my journal that it was the happiest day of my life. We even set a date to announce our intentions—October thirteenth. Now I could see that was never going to happen. So I sadly started a new page.

I love you, Johnny. Why this should be, I do not know. Today you are showing me how much I mean to you. October 13 is the day we were going to get engaged and today you aren't even going find a minute to call me. You are spending the day with some other girl of your choice. I guess you know what you're doing. Rather than tell me to get lost, you're doing it the sure way—the way you can hurt the most—break my spirit. But that's impossible. I have done the best I can do in my relationship with you, but I guess that's not good enough. I think you thought a lot of me, too, but you weren't sure of yourself, and your new girlfriend convinced you of my inadequacy. If she really wants you, you don't have to play games with me to keep her interest. Be free and open; share your dreams, share your pride, share your "evil" side. You're a wonderful guy, Johnny. Don't let anyone sell you short.

The backstory on John was that he was a cook in the kitchen in one of the pavilions of Michael Reese Hospital. All the cooks were black people as were most of the employees in the Dietary Department. I was one of the therapeutic dietitians who visited patients on special diets and planned their diet modifications. John said he took an interest in me, because I walked and talked like a country girl; and he could tell I was not from Chicago. One day he invited me to go with him to a kitchen staff party. Accepting his invitation brought me to the negative attention of my immediate supervisor, the head dietitian over our pavilion. It seems she was "sweet" on John, and she confronted me at the party saying white people weren't really welcome. However, John and his friends told me not to pay her any attention, and they proceeded to teach me how to dance one of the current dances in which you had to move your shoulders freely. I did love the music and drank a couple glasses of gin and tonic, which helped me enjoy the party in spite of my supervisor's hostility.

At work she started to monitor me so closely that she pointed out each supposed mistake every day. Eventually she took a dietary complaint from a doctor, blamed me big time, and reported to the department head that I didn't know what I was doing. He decided I should be given a competency test, which turned out to be quite simple and basic, so I was able to pass it with one hundred percent. My department head was then instructed to treat me better. After that, I really got a display of superficiality and hypocrisy. It just about made me sick how she gushed over me, and invited me to go shopping with her and go to a picnic with her. I told John's sister, Clara, about the amazing turnaround at work, and she agreed I was right to turn down her social invitations. But then Clara said she thought a picnic would be a great idea for our two families someday when the weather was good.

Two weeks after his first visit the FBI agent returned to our apartment, again on a Saturday morning. Janice had gone shopping and Rachel and the baby were sleeping late.

He began the conversation by saying apologetically, "I am so sorry, but I seem to have misplaced my notebook where I took all the notes from our conversation two weeks ago. I need to ask you some of the same questions all over again. I do apologize."

For the first time, I became suspicious of this guy. "Sir, I don't mean any disrespect, but FBI agents have to be better organized than that, don't they?"

"Actually yes, that's true. I can't believe I did that." Then he said a little too jovially, "We are human, too, you know."

He laughed. I didn't think it was funny.

He continued in a markedly more serious vein, "I really am sorry to bother you, but I need to ask your cooperation once again." He took out a notebook and pencil, and asked me some of the same questions he had asked before. I thought he might be checking to see if I gave the same answers. He had assured me on the last visit that I was not a suspect, but I got an uneasy feeling that he didn't trust me.

He looked up from his note taking. "What's the chance I could get a cup of coffee like last time? It would really hit the spot."

I left him alone in the living room again, like on his first visit. While I put together the coffee tray with milk and sugar in the kitchen, I tried to decide how I was going to tell the truth to him that I never made any calls to find out names of people as I had promised him. What stopped me from calling anyone was thinking to myself, *"How would I explain to those guys I worked with why I want their phone numbers? Do I want to go on being friends with them? That's not realistic. Do I want to tell them they are for the FBI? No, of course not."* So I made the choice not to make any calls. Now I was sure that was the right decision.

I returned in about three or four minutes saying in a straightforward manner, "You know, I never did get a chance to make any phone calls to find out phone numbers of people I met last summer."

The agent didn't seem particularly disappointed. "Oh, that's okay." Then he surprised me.

"You're going to be subpoenaed to a preliminary grand jury hearing, the purpose being to indict the people who crossed state lines to disrupt the Democratic Convention."

"What? I thought you said I wasn't a suspect." I couldn't believe my ears.

"Not you, Miss Beverly. You're going to be asked to identify Bobby Seale. That's all. He will be in the courtroom with the other suspects."

"When'll this be? I work, you know."

"I'm not sure when it'll be. You'll be notified by mail. You'll have to make arrangements to be there."

He left me with a lot of questions. I felt all alone. *With whom could I, a regular common citizen, talk about how to deal with the*

FBI? How did they track me down in the first place? Why did he pretend to lose his notebook? Did I do anything wrong or did I not? I couldn't believe how easy it was to get into trouble in the big city for doing things clearly within the law. I was just trying to be helpful, giving a speaker a ride to a peace rally.

Big city living was becoming uncomfortably different from my growing up years. I strongly felt I needed someone who would help me get some perspective on this surge of events. Getting forced into the follow-up of the clash between protesters and the Chicago government, I knew I needed to see the other side of my Democratic Convention experiences. I didn't know anyone who worked for the city, except the school policeman, but I knew that discussion was not appropriate at work. Unexpectedly, I found a city employee sitting next to me at a B.B. King performance in a downtown Chicago jazz club. I had gone alone to hear this famous blues musician in person because I couldn't find anyone to go with me. We started talking between numbers and between sets. Besides working for the Chicago city government, he told me he was a Democratic precinct captain which meant he got out the vote of the 478 Democrats in his precinct. There were only two Republicans—the Republican precinct captain and his wife. I told him I was teaching in inner-city Chicago.

I asked him what he was doing during the Democratic Convention. He said he was going to work every day, but Mayor Daley had all city workers on call that week, in case they were needed. The mayor had called his city workers together before the convention and told them, "We're not going to put up with any riots or let demonstrators destroy our neighborhoods."

I asked him, "Do you think Mayor Daley succeeded?"

"Yes, of course. Daley meant business. He called out the National Guard and the state police to work with the Chicago police to keep the peace. He kept the demonstrators from causing any major damage and disrupting the Democratic Convention. The majority of the citizens of Chicago were glad nothing spread to their neighborhoods. Yeah, he succeeded."

"Well, I think a case could be made that the war protesters were successful, too."

He waved off my remark. "Forget it. They can't both be successful."

"Maybe they weren't trying to disrupt the convention. Maybe they were just trying to get attention—television coverage—so they could sway public opinion against the war."

"Bullshit. Their motivations weren't that simple."

"No? Did you ever think maybe they were simply trying to carry out the intentions of their hero, JFK? He was leaning against the war before he was assassinated."

He let out a disbelieving laugh, "I'm not so sure about that. He was the one who first sent Americans over there."

I felt safe with him, so I kept on making my case. "Maybe the protesters were trying to show the American public the power of numbers. The young people that had to fight the war stood together against the war—they showed they could even stand up to the police power."

"I do know the mayor got us through the convention with no casualties and made the city look good to the world. He showed 'em we're the city that works."

I changed my tone to a more conciliatory one. "I appreciate talking to you, you know, because I was wondering what was behind so much police presence. Now I understand what Mayor Daley was trying to accomplish."

He asked if I wanted another gin and tonic. I declined. He ordered another drink for himself and I took another sip from mine.

"All presidents seem to get mired in wars," I continued. "Lyndon Johnson dropped out of the fray and he didn't even seek the nomination. I thought that was unfortunate. He was carrying on for JFK, you know, civil rights, voting rights, war on poverty, such important things, but his big mistake was the endless continuation of the Vietnam War."

He shook his head in agreement. "I don't really care about national politics. Like I said, at least the mayor got Chicago through the convention without casualties."

Thinking about our conversation afterward, I remembered he had said something about how the FBI helped keep the hippies from making trouble for Chicago by recording and listening to their telephone conversations. I didn't tell him about my FBI visits, but that explained the agent's odd requests for coffee. Our telephone was in the living room where I left him alone twice, once each time he came to visit. He might have installed a wiretap on his first visit and removed it on his second visit.

After I got over the shock that our apartment telephone might have been bugged, I tried to remember the conversations I had with John and other guys during that period. All I could think was that I was a case study of love unrequited. It was so pitiful, I had to either laugh or cry, imagining some agent playing the tapes and wondering if there was any hope for the younger generation. I remembered my sister's serious recommendation that I get a counselor to straighten out my life. I wondered if she might be right.

The next week I went to the Bureau of Motor Vehicles to exchange my Iowa license plate for an Illinois plate. All of a sudden, I realized how the FBI found me. It was the detective writing down my license number out at the airport. He only had that Iowa license to go by, and the car was registered to my brother who gave our home address—the folks' home—as his permanent address while in college. I had bought the car from my brother for one hundred dollars when he went overseas.

I called my folks to see if anyone had contacted them about my Iowa license plate. My mother put my dad on the line. Dad told me with a shaking voice that an FBI agent came out to talk to him in the field where Dad was driving the tractor cultivating corn, and all the agent asked him was who was driving the car with the Iowa license plate. He didn't tell my dad if I was in trouble or not, only that they were trying to find the driver to ask some questions. I apologized for not telling him and Mom that I had driven the car out to the airport to pick up a speaker for the antiwar protests at the Democratic Convention. Then I told him the whole story. He listened stoically. It was tense.

I have never been able to imagine what fears my dad and mom must have had, and how many sleepless nights it may have caused them. It made me angry. I thought again as I did that day in the airport, *Why couldn't the FBI guy just ask me my name and address right there at the airport?* I would have told him. I guess that would have been too simple, too straightforward.

Who would have guessed that it would be my mother and father in rural Iowa who had to suffer emotionally when I tried to do something simple in Chicago to take a stand against the war? What a chain of unlikely events.

All seemed to be forgotten and forgiven when one day I received an urgent phone call from my parents, asking if I could get in contact with anyone like a lawyer in the antiwar movement about my brother. It seems Erwin's two-year nonmilitary assignment was to end in Laos in December of 1968. He just received a letter from the US Selective Service System, which again ordered him to appear in front of the draft board of Floyd County, Iowa. It explained that although he had been classified as a conscientious objector (due to his being against killing people in Vietnam), his two-year deferral from the armed services was coming to an end.

My parents felt that two years as a conscientious objector teaching agriculture in the remote rural areas of southern Laos where he was dangerously close to the strongholds of the Pathet Lao, lawless communist terrorists like the Viet Cong, more than equaled two years of serving in the US Army as a soldier. My parents contacted the local draft board and made their case, but the answer was, "The law is the law!" Erwin was required to return from southeast Asia to Charles City, Iowa for his military classification to be changed to "1-A" and then be sent to Vietnam. Daunted by the military decision, my parents still wanted us as a family to do what we could to help Erwin to maintain his status in alternative service. I agreed to see what I could do.

While I looked for a letter I had just received from Erwin, I remembered the folks telling me that sometimes the Pathet Lao would send a message to his village Houei Kong that they were going to come into town that night and kill the American. He worked it out with local villagers that one of them would go into hiding with him in the surrounding jungle. The villagers would be armed, but EJ, as they called him in Laos, couldn't be armed, because he was a conscientious objector working for a pacifist agency. I always wondered how anyone could sleep in conditions like that. What if someone snored? I found Erwin's letter, read it again, and was amazed again.

It has all been very chaotic lately. Two weeks ago a jeep came barreling down one of the laterite roads in the jungle. It hit a land mine under the road. It was probably placed there by the Pathet Lao. Several people were seriously hurt, including a Catholic missionary priest. The local medics in the village didn't have the equipment or training to deal with the severely wounded. The medics ran to my office to see if I could evacuate the wounded via military chopper to the Filipino Operation Brotherhood Hospital located in the village of Paksong about 30 miles from Houei Kong. The option of sending them back to Paksong via the road they had just traveled was unthinkable, because of their wounds and the danger of another mine. So I got out my black box (a special Mayday radio) and called for support. I was successful in summoning a helicopter to take those with critical wounds to the Paksong hospital. Then, I got an urgent call that the chopper was returning to Houie Kong to pick me up and take me to the Paksong hospital. The priest desperately needed blood and the doctors knew that my blood was O positive (a universal donor), because I had previously been treated for a wound at the hospital. I ended up giving blood directly to the priest whose need was so imperative that the doctors hooked us up via a tube. I watched my blood flow to the priest. They stopped the flow after guessing that I gave him a pint and a half. The priest survived, suffering only the partial loss of one of his legs.

My parents asked me if I could find out if Erwin had any recourse other than to automatically follow the orders of the local draft board. I couldn't help appreciating the irony of this situation. Earlier they disapproved of my participation in the antiwar movement during the Democratic Convention, but now my connections with people in the antiwar movement became useful and even indispensable to get justice for their conscientious objector son.

I was confident that the antiwar movement people would have the answers for EJ. My first call was fruitful. I was told I needed to meet with William Kunstler, the top lawyer involved in defending protesters who had been arrested and incarcerated during the Democratic Convention. I was given the number of his hotel room so I could call him. It surprised me how accessible and trusting antiwar people were. It seemed the way it should be in a peaceable world.

Mister Kunstler met me in the hotel lobby. I recognized him from pictures in the newspapers. As I walked toward him, he stood up from sitting very relaxed in an easy chair, shook my hand, and invited me to sit in a chair facing him.

"How can I help you?"

"This is so nice of you to take time to meet with me. I can't even imagine how busy you are. I need advice for my brother, EJ. He's been serving as a conscientious objector over in Laos for two years and the local Iowa draft board says he must now come home, get his classification changed, and join the army."

"Well now, that's what this movement is all about. I always make time for a man putting his life on the line to resist the war. Tell me a little more about him."

"EJ graduated in June 1965 from Iowa State College in Agriculture Education. The Floyd County draft board was put in a conundrum about his refusal to kill anyone. They reluctantly assigned him as a conscientious objector to two years in the International Voluntary Service. You probably know about IVS."

"I sure do. It's a Quaker organization that provides a government-approved alternative to military service."

"So now that he has almost put in his two years in Laos, the local draft board aims to draft him for the military since his deferral is coming to an end. That's not fair."

"No, it's not. Help me clarify the timeline here. He graduated in 1965. How old is your brother now?"

"Let's see. Twenty-four. He'll be twenty-five in December."

Mister Kunstler smiled and slapped his hands on his knees. "Perfect. They almost never draft anyone after their 26th birthday. What your brother needs to do is start the appeals process. He can do that from Laos. The first appeal is to the county draft board and that process takes up to twelve months. When he loses that appeal, and he will, he appeals to the state. The state appeal takes twelve months. That will make him almost twenty-seven; he'll be home free."

A great wave of relief swept over me. I asked incredulously, "Is it really that easy?"

"Nothing is ever easy when you're dealing with Uncle Sam's wars. While his appeals are playing out, he needs to stay overseas. If he returns home, he'll lose his right to appeal. It would probably be best for him to stay in Laos. That's an important service he's doing for the people over there, right?"

"Right. He's teaching year-round rice farming using irrigation to subsistence farmers."

"Can he serve another two years with IVS?"

"I don't really know, but I know he'll figure something out." I stood up. "I can't thank you enough. How much do I owe you?"

"Not one cent. I'm the one to thank you. I love to meet people who are really committed to peacemaking in the world. You remind me why I'm involved in this work. Good luck to you."

I felt like leaping in the air as I left the hotel. The whole meeting probably took less than twenty minutes, but it might save Erwin's life.

I couldn't wait a moment longer. I went back into the hotel lobby, found a pay phone, and called the folks collect. I could hear their sighs of relief. My mother didn't think he could serve any longer with IVS, but EJ knew some people working for US AID (United States Agency for International Development), who said they could probably get him into that agency.

CHAPTER 5
Black Is Beautiful

WINTER, 1969

"Black is beautiful" was a popular phrase, which I often heard spoken among African American students. I looked for chances to apply this concept in the classroom without being preachy. Having attended the Ebony Fashion Show at McCormick Place sponsored by Johnson, Publishers of *Ebony Magazine*, I got ideas for the launch of a fashion show we could have in the spring. I contacted Ebony publishers and they offered to send us a consultant to teach the students to do modeling steps. I had the consultant approved as an "outside speaker," and she led a workshop in each of my clothing classes. The students were awestruck. They loved practicing the quarter turn, the half turn, and especially the whole 360 degree turn. They even learned to stand straight, shoulders back and tummy in, to improve their posture.

Reverend Jesse Jackson, founder of Operation Push, was doing outreach to black teenagers during those years. He had some thought-provoking advice which I would post on the bulletin boards. In those moments at the end of class periods when we were waiting for the passing bell, I would bring them up to try to get discussion going:

- A father is not someone who can make a baby. A father is a man who can raise a baby.

- If my mind can conceive it and I can believe it, then I can achieve it.

- Excuses bring you sympathy, not success.

I started wondering why half of the students in my classes, regardless of race, would apply themselves to the subjects at hand, do their homework, and study for tests. The other half had ingenious excuses. Half of them had almost perfect attendance; the rest had many absences, which I was required to document. If they brought no excuse, then I was to call parents. For all absentees, I was to provide makeup work (which very few absentees completed and turned in.) Lots of my time went into accommodating the erratic students with little return for the effort.

At the end of the first marking period I decided to grade quite strictly, not giving the benefit of the doubt. This was in hopes of shaping up the errant students. The day they received their grades, one group of five or six angry students marched into my classroom after ninth period. "You failed me. You don't like black people," one accused me. "You're prejudiced," another complained loudly.

My answer just came out and I surprised myself as much as them by saying confidently, "Yes, I am prejudiced. I'm prejudiced against students who don't do their homework assignments or their classroom work for that matter."

"We DID do all our work."

"Well, let's see the record book." I opened the book to the classroom roster and grade record sheet dramatically. "Who wants to go first? We'll look up your name right here and see what's recorded. If there're no zeroes, then I'm wrong. But if there are a number of zeroes, then you're wrong."

The first one who wanted to see her record was one of the worst/best examples to make my point. There were more zeroes than there were grades of A, B, C, or D. We also looked at her attendance record, and found that there was at least one absence every week. "Okay, who's next?" I asked.

The record of the second volunteer was almost identical. I told them that I assigned homework and class work for a reason—so they would learn. I challenged them to get a fresh start the next marking period—to study and learn. They marched out of the classroom accusing each other of giving in.

When I called home about absences, more than once I found that the family didn't have enough pairs of boots or winter coats for all of their children to go to school every day. Two children sometimes had to share one pair of boots. One would have them one day, the other another day. In those cases, it was relatively simple for me to go buy what they needed at a thrift store or to find donations, and it did solve that problem temporarily. In other cases, a high school girl had to stay at home to care for preschool brothers and sisters when the mother had a doctor's appointment. That was a harder situation to solve, but I was glad that the Armitage Avenue Methodist Church had started the free child care program in the basement where we had the summer school. I could refer them. I discovered, however, in far too many cases the students were cutting class. They had reported to division for their school attendance, but not to my class. Sometimes I felt I was a failure, because I couldn't motivate them all to want to study and learn.

After I did the best I could with each and every student, and those techniques did work with some of them, I concluded that it must be family support or lack of support that made the biggest difference. Sometimes when I would call parents, they would ask with resignation, "But how can I get them to do their homework?" or even "How can I get them to come home after school?"

Once I asked a mother how often they had family dinner

together. I had begun to suspect this might be part of the effectiveness puzzle. Classroom foods teaching revealed to me how much organization goes into meal preparation for a family sit-down meal. And, if you have not been brought up in a family practicing this, I suspected its value might not be appreciated. So, for the rest of my years teaching home economics, I encouraged daily family dinners together every chance I got. I told the girls, "The experience of sitting at a table with your lab partners (or your family) provides wonderful opportunities to work together, to get to talk and listen to each other, and share ideas and daily life events."

I don't know why I was surprised that another major difference I observed between many successful and unsuccessful students was church attendance. I found that if the family attended church together, the students seemed to have adopted values that also supported their success in school, such as good attendance, respectfulness, honesty, kindness, responsibility, and trying to be the best person they could be. I didn't recommend church attendance to students or their families, because of my understanding of the separation of church and state; however, whenever I heard them talking about going to church, I would say, "Very good."

At the end of the first semester, students in another one of my classes accused me of prejudice when they got their grades and I used the same technique to demonstrate the cause of their bad grades was their own choice to not do assignments. This time, I decided to face the topic of prejudice head-on. I ordered a movie entitled *Prejudice* through the Bureau of Visual Education to show in class. In college, I learned that we should always preview movies before showing them to students. In real life teaching, I found it very difficult to get the movie projector and the movie to be previewed at the same time, as I had my one free period to sit and look at it in an empty classroom. That's why I showed this movie sight unseen in the troubled class, and was dismayed with the content.

It was an old black and white movie about two groups of European immigrant students—Italian and Irish—and how their prejudice toward each other played out in a New York City neighborhood. I was upset, because I didn't think it was appropriate for my students at all due to the age of the movie and how it wasn't about prejudice based on skin color, but on ethnic hatred among whites that went back generations. I didn't think it would mean anything to the black and Hispanic students.

However the students were mesmerized as they watched the movie in complete silence. Afterwards, when I started to apologize to them, they surprised me by unanimously agreeing with the student who said, "It was a good flick. We didn't know there was any other kind of prejudice besides whites against blacks."

One student asked, "Are some white people really prejudiced against other white people?"

"Yes, they are."

"Were you prejudiced against, Miss Johnson?" I was put on the spot. Uncomfortable sharing about my own life, I took a deep breath and told them anyway, "I grew up on an Iowa farm. When I went to town school in first grade, the town kids made fun of me and all of us country kids. We were all white, but they mostly had store-bought clothes and we had homemade clothes. I knew in my heart they were no better than us, but it hurt to be looked down upon."

Another student shared an insight. "Some people always want to feel superior to others, and they will find any old reason, no matter what race they are."

I found it most satisfying to explore a topic with students for which I did not have ready-made answers. I remembered learning in college to differentiate between inductive and deductive reasoning, and I realized that inductive teaching was a good way to get the students involved in group problem solving and to develop reasoning skills. The outcome was uncertain, especially with a complicated, even controversial, topic. But this experiment helped me further develop my own style of teaching. I discovered I loved to see students actively involved in their own learning.

It was some of the coldest days of Chicago winter when the Chicago Teachers Union called the first strike in its history. It put me in a serious dilemma. I had to figure out whether I was going to join the strike or not. I had only been teaching for four months and hadn't yet joined the teachers' union. It seemed wrong and perilous to refuse to report to work, and it seemed equally problematic to work when everyone else was on strike. Checking with my parents, they said they were opposed to unions and strikes. I told them the truth as to why I was thinking of joining the union, because one teacher told me stories of how it used to be.

"You would join the union if you knew what conditions were like before we had a union. Often the Board of Education said they didn't have enough money to pay teachers their last paycheck of the year right before Christmas, so they gave us IOU notes. Another Christmas, they gave us extra days off. They treat teachers like day laborers, who should show our love for children by never expecting raises in pay."

I reluctantly decided I needed to strike with the teachers even though I knew my mother was disappointed in me. I tried to explain the reasons to her. She said she would try to keep an open mind toward this part of working in the city.

The day I joined the union was the day the strike began. January 1969 was one of the coldest months of a very cold Chicago winter. One teacher who lived in the Lincoln Park neighborhood brought a barrel and started a fire in it. When we got cold as we marched around the school building, we could go warm our hands over the fire. We teachers got a chance to talk informally and, in general, we had a good time. One benefit for me was getting to know more teachers outside my department and to feel as though I was becoming an integral part of the teaching team of Waller High School.

After about two weeks, the Board of Education relented and gave teachers a raise. It was about equivalent to the money we lost while on strike. I learned later that other salary issues such as pay scales and classroom conditions were addressed in negotiations between the teachers union and the school board, and a grievance procedure was instituted to prevent future strikes.

It was surreal, the daily ritual of reading the newspaper headlines and articles about what was dubbed as the Conspiracy Eight grand jury selection, the preliminaries, and the hearing itself. I knew full well that I would have to play a part in the courtroom drama someday because of the ride I gave to Bobby Seale from the airport to Lincoln Park.

And what a drama it was. The defendants were usually listed in alphabetical order: Rennie Davis, David Dellinger, John Froines, Tom Hayden, Abbie Hoffman, Jerry Rubin, Bobby Seale, and Lee Weiner. They were charged with conspiring together to start a riot during the Democratic Convention and crossing state lines to carry out their planned riot. There was plenty of press coverage now, and it appeared that all the actors in the drama were exaggerating their parts. The white guys played the Yippie role, making fun of Judge Julius Hoffman and the government lawyers by wisecracking, laughing, and shouting obscenities. Judge Hoffman repeatedly stated he was determined to conduct his court in a hard line, strict, no nonsense way.

Bobby Seale was different from the other defendants. Besides being the only black man in the courtroom, it was obviously no game for him. He refused to cooperate with the judge and the lawyers, saying over and over that he didn't belong there. He insisted he had a right to be represented by his own lawyer, but his California lawyer was recovering from surgery at the time.

The dreaded day arrived when I received an official-looking document in the mail telling me I was summoned by subpoena to appear at the grand jury hearing the next week. My attendance was required, and there would be consequences, if I did not comply. The school principal, Doctor Amar, excused me without question.

I didn't have time to get nervous. Before I knew it, I was sitting in the witness chair, vowing to tell the truth. The government prosecutor clarified my presence at the demonstration on August 27, 1968. Then I was asked if I could point out Bobby Seale in the courtroom. I said, "Yes."

Bobby was sitting, slouched down in his chair, glowering at no one in particular. When I pointed him out, our eyes met briefly. He did not seem angry at me. I'm guessing he was just despondent at the whole situation in which he found himself. I had expected more questions, but I was abruptly excused. I heard Bobby yell as I walked out that he had a right to his own lawyer, and he was not doing or saying anything without his lawyer.

On March 20, 1969, the federal grand jury returned indictments against the Chicago Eight demonstration leaders, including Bobby

Seale, and also against eight police officers. I learned from television and the newspaper that they called in more than two hundred witnesses during the almost six months of the grand jury hearings which began in October. The full trial was scheduled to begin the next September. I thought, *Oh, Lordy, I will have to appear again for questioning. Well, I can't dwell on it. "What will be will be."*

CHAPTER 6

Riot or Revolution?

APRIL 4, 1969

As I walked into the teachers' lunchroom for my usual early morning cup of coffee, a teacher came over to me with a very serious demeanor.

"Bev, you better get up to your classroom. Some students are throwing chairs in the student lunchroom. There's going to be trouble in school today."

I felt a knot in my throat, "What's wrong?"

"Martin Luther King was shot a year ago today. Just hurry. The students will tell you the rest."

In my classroom, about twelve students were huddled with wide fear-filled eyes. One student begged, "Can my brother stay here with me?"

"My sister, too," another pleaded. "They're afraid to go to their classes."

"Miss Johnson, this is a bad riot. Kids are running through the hallways in the old building with squirt guns, fire extinguishers, and baseball bats, smashing lockers and stair railings. It's awful."

I tried to collect my thoughts. *Beverly, this is Chicago, not Iowa. Expect it to be different.* Throughout my brief teaching career, that self-talk kept me from shocking easily and helped me switch from uncertainty to strong teacher mode. I realized I had better forget the rules that only enrolled students were allowed in a classroom.

I mustered my in-charge voice. "Okay, you can stay here. I'll lock the door, and we'll be careful who we let in. Let's make this room a safe place for as long as need be."

I asked, "Have there ever been riots like this in Waller High School before?"

"Yes, exactly a year ago today when Martin Luther King was shot and killed. My mama said we would always remember the date April 4, 1968."

I welcomed about twenty other kids who said they were scared of the violence. Students who were in my classroom talked among themselves about King. I realized for the first time the depth of anger and despair in the black community after the assassination of their hero and beloved leader. They spoke of Martin Luther King's teachings and how their parents and churches adored him.

"Miss Johnson, why do they have to kill all the good people who are trying to help us? Not only Martin Luther King, but there was President Kennedy, then his brother, Robert Kennedy."

Another student said, "Yeah, and Malcolm X."

"I don't know, girls. Those are good questions that haunt me, too."

I told them how I went to hear Martin Luther King speak in the Chicago Coliseum when he came to Chicago to lead a civil rights march in Cicero, a southwestern suburb of Chicago. Cicero was widely considered one of the most segregated northern cities. My friend, Anna Mae, and I went outside to the back of the auditorium after the speech. We hoped to see him up close as he left to get into his limousine, but he didn't come out that way. He must have gone out a different way, because of concerns for his safety.

I did not tell them how many times I heard people say that Martin Luther King must be communist, because J. Edgar Hoover was investigating him. King was criticized for causing riots. It wasn't until my senior year in college that they started a campus organization called SCORE (Student Committee on Racial Equality.) I learned first-hand about the need to improve race relations in America. A boyfriend and I joined an open housing march around the Iowa state capitol. We even got our picture in the newspaper. All these flashbacks went through my mind that long school day in which we barricaded ourselves in my clothing classroom.

The riot didn't end until the dismissal bell of the school day. All of a sudden, it was announced over the loudspeaker that teachers and students were to leave the building. The students left my safe room class, as relieved and as thankful as I was.

About a week later, I decided to go visit a friend and former co-worker who just had her first baby in Michael Reese Hospital. My car was in the shop, so I caught a taxi. On the ride from the near north side of Chicago to the near south side, I got into a prophetic conversation with the black taxi driver.

He asked me, "What did'ya think of the riots in Chicago last week?"

"They were bad news, weren't they? A lot of people were really angry. I guess they didn't know what else to do with their anger."

"There'll never be another Martin Luther King. I hear tell they're thinking of renaming this here South Park Boulevard, and calling it Martin Luther King Drive."

"Martin Luther King was a great man. He could have been elected president if he wanted to."

"You honestly think so? I always wondered who would be president first—a black man or a white woman?"

I answered, "Oh, a black man, of course."

He responded, "No, I don't think so. It'll be a white woman."

"I'll tell you one thing. We'll never know the answer to that one in our lifetimes."

"You got that right."

It was the final marking period and students were finalizing their clothing construction projects. Several of them would soon have outfits they could wear in the practice fashion show. The Foods and Nutrition classes knew how to make cookies and beverages suitable for refreshments.

I spoke to them about inviting a few guests, "There have been some teachers who are really interested in your work. Maybe some of your parents could come, too. You all would be able to see each other's work. Everyone could practice their modeling turns in front of a small audience. It will be like a dress rehearsal for putting on a real fashion show during the next school year."

Not very many people came, but we did the practice fashion show one lab class period as planned. Afterwards, during punch and cookie time in the classroom, there was unanimous agreement that we should give a real full-fledged fashion show next year. I started a sign-up sheet for students who would like to model or help with refreshments. Because models had to be in clothing classes, it looked like my class size would double with aspiring seamstress-models. Boys signed up, too, telling me they were going to elect home economics next year. That would mean the end of all-girl classes in home economics.

It was a time of self-awareness for me, a young first-year teacher, now feeling more like a genuine city and country girl. I had been willing to take risks and face the challenges of understanding differences, as well as identifying similarities among black, white,

Asian, and Hispanic students. Peacemaking was shaping up as a major theme in my life. I had a new vision of a peaceful world where all races and nationalities could live and work together in harmony.

Achieving tenure was a lot more than putting in time as a teacher. There was a three-part test and I had to pass each part before going on to the next part. The first part was general knowledge and basic skills test of mathematics and English. A teacher in the school where I worked lent me his study booklet and I read it from cover to cover. I actually got one hundred percent, so I imagined they were expecting great things from me for the next two tests. They didn't get them.

Part two was a written test over field of specialty. Home economics included foods and nutrition, textiles and clothing, child development, family living, home management, and psychological and biological sciences. I passed with a score of eighty-five percent. Part three was a practical exam. Mine was in food preparation. Teachers forewarned me we had to make a white sauce from scratch and from memory. Then there was a menu we had to prepare, and everything had to be ready to serve at exactly the same time, attractively presented, hot things hot and cold things cold. I was nervous as I reported to the foods lab for this last requirement because organization is not my greatest strength even though I liked to cook. I was the last to complete the assignment a little after the time limit and I ended up with a few tenths of a point below the 75 percent minimum. The three tests were averaged, my basic skills test carried me over, and I passed the three-part test.

After that ordeal, the final step toward achieving tenure was an interview with a panel of principals and administrators at the central offices of the Chicago school system. I dressed in my best two-piece suit and blouse. Back then, I machine-sewed all of my clothing, including coats, but that wasn't what I was tested on nor did I get any credit for my sewing abilities.

I wasn't really nervous about this last step of the tenure process until I walked into the interview room. The principals and central office administrators who sat on my interview team were six middle-aged men and women in a row at a long table. Preoccupied with folders and piles of papers in front of them, they didn't acknowledge my presence. There was one empty chair in the middle of the room about eight feet away from them facing their table. One of the interviewers looked up, motioned me to take the solitary chair. I felt isolated and very alone, soon to be the center of complete strangers' attention, like on a firing line.

Their initial questions began as soon as I acknowledged being Beverly Johnson. "Could you tell us about the job you had before coming to Chicago?"

"I was a short-term missionary for three-and-a half-years with the Methodist Church. I worked as a hospital dietitian and taught normal nutrition and diet therapy in a nurse's training school at Sanatorio Palmore, a hospital located in Chihuahua, Mexico."

"Do you still consider yourself a missionary?"

"In a way."

"Oh, really?" another interviewer asked as he pushed back in his chair. "In what way do you consider yourself a missionary working in a public school system?"

I took a moment to select my words. "Teaching seems like a mission in itself. I've found the young people in Chicago have a lot of needs, not only educational, but physical and social. So many of them have never even ventured outside their neighborhoods into the big world out there."

Some of the interviewers wrote something down. I wondered what they found interesting in that answer.

Another interviewer cleared his throat. "Let's see here. Did you go to a church-related college?"

"No, I went to a public land grant college—Iowa State College of Science and Technology."

"I see. But for the last almost four years you've been working for the Methodist Church?"

"Yes."

"Well then, aren't you finding it difficult to change from a religious occupation to a secular one?"

"Not really."

"No? How can you separate the two?"

I couldn't believe the question so I hesitated.

He continued. "Aren't you going to teach your students about God? Or put up bulletin boards about God's commandments?"

"No, not in a public school."

"What if the students don't know about God? Isn't it your obligation as a missionary to tell them?"

"I won't know if they know about God or not, I guess, because we won't be talking about God in the first place."

"Okay. You seem to understand the constitutional concept of separation of church and state."

Another person whom I assumed was the head of the committee smiled at me for the first time and said, "Are you aware that in an interview such as this one, one of the members of the panel has to ask the difficult questions? It was Mister Smith's turn. He's not really a bad guy." They all laughed politely. I tried to smile back even though I was still taken aback by the line of questioning.

The whole interview lasted about ten minutes. As I walked out of the room, my legs felt like they wanted to buckle under beneath me. I took a deep breath and said to myself, *what in the world just happened to me? I surely didn't expect anything like that.* I thought they would ask me about my first year teaching or maybe my students. I wondered if the separation of church and state had been a problem in the public schools.

I walked back into the waiting room where there were now five male teachers sitting and waiting. One black guy asked, "How'd it go?"

"I'm not sure. It was weird."

"Oh, don't worry. You'll pass. Look what color you are."

"I wish it was that easy."

With that sarcastic inference, my morning was complete; I felt poked, prodded, and shot at. I thought how teaching in the Chicago Public Schools is not for the faint of heart. You have to really want to be there for the kids, or you better get out.

I looked at the other guys. I couldn't believe my eyes. Sitting next to the guy with the chip on his shoulder was my summer '68 co-worker, Carlos, all slicked up with short hair, wearing a dress shirt and formal tie. I had never seen him looking like that. He jumped up and came bounding toward me. We hugged, as Latinos always do, ending the hug with a handshake.

"What're you doing here?" I asked him. "I thought you were supposed to be in Puerto Rico."

"It's a long story. Do ya have time to wait around for me? I think I'm next."

"Sure. Of course. I'd love to hear your story."

Just then someone called for Carlos Ortiz. I said, "Good luck in there."

✹

I left the waiting room and went over to a big window in the vestibule outside the elevators. The window overlooked the

Chicago River. The trees on either side of the river had the fresh green leaves of spring. This looked so much better than the endless graying snow of winter. The central offices were in the Builders Building facing upper Wacker Drive in the downtown Loop. I had made several trips here during the year to complete application requirements and take required tests toward tenure culminating with this interview.

My mind wandered to Carlos, remembering he was going to go stay with his aunt and uncle in Puerto Rico and work for the independence movement. He said the government was going to have a referendum this spring. He was against the other choices on the referendum, which were statehood or continuation as a free-associated commonwealth. I wondered how that worked out.

Carlos came out of the interview smiling as he always did. We took the elevator down and walked out of the Board of Education building and crossed the La Salle Street Bridge over the Chicago River. A new restaurant had outdoor tables overlooking the river. We ordered *café con leche,* which came right away.

Carlos inhaled the aroma, making a satisfying sound before he took a sip.

"Bev, I have a confession to make." He took a slow deep breath and let it out. "I lied. I don't know why I told everyone that I was going to Puerto Rico this year. The truth is I went there the summer of '67."

"What? I don't understand. Why lie?"

"I can't really explain it. I guess I thought it sounded better. I didn't want the students to hear about how I was a complete failure on the island."

"You mean about the referendum? So what happened for real?"

"I tried my best to convince people for independence. I studied all sides of the issues and I thought I presented 'em convincingly.

But I don't think I changed one single person's mind. I was actually angry how the vote came out. They voted to keep the government just like it is. It's been like that ever since independence from Spain in 1898. Can you believe it?"

"Maybe politics is not your thing. Anyway, how did the vote pan out?"

"The status quo won easily. Our generation was about the only people who wanted independence. They dismissed us as revolutionaries. The second highest vote was for statehood."

"Did the kids in our summer program understand the differences in the three options?"

"Truthfully? I don't think they cared. Mainland kids born here don't feel much of a connection with the island. So, that's why I decided to focus more on Latino Pride with them, being proud of who they are and what they can become. I could see that meant a lot to them. And art speaks louder than words."

"Yeah, they held their heads higher at the end of the summer than at the beginning, thanks to you, Carlos."

"Funny you should say that, Bev. I've never forgotten how Reverend Johnson, Bruce, convinced me I was good at teaching. He told me the kids admired me, especially how I finished high school and took classes at City College. He said I should be proud that every single kid in our summer program went on to high school this past fall in a time, when less than fifty percent of Latinos finish high school, less than any other group."

"So are you thinking about teaching high school?"

"No, I wanna teach fifth grade. There aren't many men teaching in middle schools. Look at all those kids without fathers. They need role models. It starts in middle school—most boys adopt the attitude that it's not cool to study or enjoy learning. Those are the ones I know I can reach. So here I am taking the big step to get my teaching certificate."

We sipped our coffee in silence for a moment, looking out at a barge and tow boat on the river. Carlos broke the silence.

"You might be interested in something else. Do ya know what else I've been doing this year until just now?"

"Heavens no, I can't even guess."

"Working with the YLO"

"What's that?"

"Young Lords Organization."

"Oh, yeah. I almost forgot about them, even though I've been teaching all year in Waller High School right in the middle of Lincoln Park. Are you kidding? You became a Young Lord?"

"No, no, no. But anyway, they're not a street gang anymore. They've gone straight arrow. That way I've been able to work with 'em without joining 'em. Bruce is working with 'em, too. It's been a wild year."

"What's been happening?"

"Okay, are you ready for all this? The YLO staged an occupation of Peoples Park for four months and they actually prevented the city from turning the lot on the corner of Armitage and Halsted into tennis courts. I helped about three hundred and fifty community volunteers get thousands of signatures on petitions. The point was to try to convince the city to zone for an apartment building for the people who once lived there above the store fronts. They even got the money to get it done by holding a seven-day takeover of McCormick Seminary. The outcome of that was to convince the seminary to donate $650,000 to build a low-income housing apartment building right on the site of the Peoples Park."

"I have seen the city tearing down old stores and cleaning up the lot."

"That reminds me I need to make a phone call. I'll be right back. Wait right there." He took off in a hurry. I didn't remember Carlos being so talkative. He seemed to thoroughly enjoy telling me about his amazing experiences. When he came back to the table, he didn't miss a beat.

"Yeah. The YLO didn't have much success trying to recruit other gangs to their serious minded goals. So they took on the city government and continued to push for day care centers, so women could go to work to support their families. Cha-Cha Jimenez announced he's gonna run in the upcoming primaries for alderman against the 'machine candidate.' He doesn't expect to win, but he wants to get enough votes on Election Day to scare the hell out of the machine. He's dressing like a politician … "

The waitress came over and asked if we wanted more coffee. We declined, paid her, and walked out together. I told him I was driving and offered to drop him off. Once I eased into traffic, I asked, "How did your interview go?"

"Very good, I think. It helps when you go to City College. We don't have to go through all the hoops you probably had to go through. It's all covered in our classes. The college placement office gets me a teaching job when I'm in my third year. In the interview, they liked it that I'm bilingual. Did they like it that you're bilingual, Bev?"

"Man, oh man. I didn't even think to tell 'em. Maybe they assumed it, since I told 'em I worked in Mexico for three and a half years."

"Don't assume anything, kid. You better take that test to get your bilingual certification. You never know how it might help you."

"Yikes. I can't even think about more testing. I've had enough for now. I'm all tested out."

Carlos threw up his hands and laughed. "Take it, amiga. You'll pass it easy."

"Maybe. I'll tell the principal at Waller High School though. It might be helpful for something."

"Yeah, like helping out some new immigrant kids who don't speak English. Do you know how hard it is for them to be in a school and not be able to understand what's going on? So how do'ya like teaching at Waller?"

"I love it. I've never been so busy in my life." I told him about seeing the summer school kids from time to time and about the day of riots.

We reached his apartment. "Carlos, before you go, I wanna tell you I never forgot that conversation we had last summer when you told me that if I didn't join the revolution, then I had to join the establishment. Do you still feel that way?"

"Y'know, no. A lot's happened since then. I think I've learned it's not either-or. Just 'cause you become part of the system doesn't mean you have to go along with their way of thinking. I'm finding out it's easier to make changes when you're working from within. There's a lot more choices every day than just revolution versus status quo."

"Truthfully, I think teachers might have the best of both worlds—we can share what we've learned with kids who need to know about life and yet we make enough money to live our own lives independently the way we want to."

"Bev, I hate to say it, but it sounds like you're growing up. How old are you again?"

"Most kids think thirty-year-olds are over-the-hill." We both laughed heartily.

"Well, that's too bad. I can hardly believe it, but you got ten years on me." Carlos reached over and gave me a little good-bye hug.

"Hey. This's been great catching up with you."

"Let's try to stay in touch, okay?"

He scribbled a phone number on a corner of some paper, tore it off and handed it to me.

"Good luck."

"Buena suerte."

I watched him disappear around the side entrance of the apartment building. I was glad he had been part of my life and sincerely hoped I would see him again.

On the way home I remembered my only male elementary teacher, a science teacher named Mister Shipley. One class period he posed a question for a small group of us students to ponder: If a tree falls in a forest and there is nobody within hearing distance, is there any sound? I could still see him smiling with a twinkle in his eye as he refused to answer the question for us. He made me think. I now knew that is what effective teaching is all about.

CHAPTER 7

War Vets

ONE WEEK BEFORE MEMORIAL DAY, 1969

I needed to take my Ford in for a tune up, including an oil change and lubrication to get it ready for a trip to Iowa. Memorial Day was to be a big day. EJ and his bride named Yoshiko were going to call the folks on the day they were to be married in the American embassy in Vientiane, Laos. My two sisters and I wanted with all our hearts to be there when the call came in.

As I waited in the auto mechanic shop, I struck up a conversation with the shop owner's son, telling him about my brother doing alternative service in Laos.

"I bought this car from my brother for one hundred dollars before he went overseas."

He said, "It's in good shape for being twelve years old. Better shape than I am. I'm not in Vietnam 'cause of physical disability." He laughed heartily and I saw he probably weighed three or four hundred pounds.

I blurted out, "Are you a 4-F just because of obesity?"

"You're right."

"I'm sorry. That was none of my business to ask that."

"Don't worry about it. By the way, the mechanic working on your car did his stint in Vietnam. Glad we could give him a job.

He came home not long ago with an honorable discharge, but he feels he can't tell no one."

"Why?"

"There's so much antiwar sentiment."

I realized the mechanic would have been listening to our conversation, since he was only ten or twelve feet away from us. I went over to the side of my car where he was working under the hood.

"I apologize for the way I was talking. It's just I'm really proud of my brother for the way he stood up against the war and became a conscientious objector, but I never met anyone who served in the military in Vietnam and came home to talk about it."

"Yeah, I was lucky," he looked up from under the hood. "I never gave it much thought at the time. I was drafted. I went. I did what I had to do. I thought I was doing the right thing."

I didn't want to say anything against that, so I asked a question, "What do'ya think now?"

He took a moment to think. "I don't know; the more I hear about this war, it makes me feel more mixed up. I do wonder why we should be fighting. But when you're over there, you don't hear anything about the government and politics. You just follow your orders, and hope you'll get through each day alive."

"My two uncles served in World War II. I know they both questioned if they were doing the right thing afterwards, and they still do. My Uncle Leslie was a pilot in the Air Force and actually dropped bombs on cities in Italy. He just recently took a trip to Italy to see the cities he bombed. I guess his hope was to see how they survived and were rebuilt."

"What'd he find?"

"He said there were still some piles of rubble, but there were gardens and new buildings and old buildings that weren't damaged."

"Didn't you say you had two uncles in the war? What about the other one?"

"I don't know anything about my Uncle Carl's service in the war. I know he was totally against the war, because he said Germany lost almost a whole generation of young men in the First World War. Maybe if those men had been able to live out their lives, they woulda been in positions of power, and coulda put a stop to the movement that swept Hitler into power and their country into the Second World War."

The mechanic tested the oil level and put on a cover, then pulled his head out and stood up facing me. "You said your Uncle Carl was against the war, but he still went when he was drafted— right? He musta felt he had to, like I did. The United States has real enemies in this world. In World War II, there was Hitler and the Japanese bombed Hawaii. If we don't go to war against our enemies that attack us, what do we do? Let them take over the world? How do we defend ourselves, if we don't fight?"

I couldn't answer his questions, because I hadn't thought them through. I felt like I was bumbling when I said, "There still has to be another way besides giving in and going to war. I think the Peace Corps is one way, and what my brother is doing is like Peace Corps. He's winning people over by working side by side with them to make a better life for everyone."

The mechanic said, "It takes a lot of guts to do what your brother's doing. It takes a lot of guts to do what I did. But it still feels terrible to come home and have to be ashamed for doing the thing required of me."

"You are giving me a lot to think about. In my opinion, you and my brother each did something different about the war, but you both did honorable duty for our country."

"You gave me something to think about, too. I have two younger brothers in school yet. I'm gonna ask the priest about them being conscientious objectors—is that what they're called?"

That night I decided to call my Uncle Carl Johnson. I wanted to see if he would tell me a little about his military service during the Second World War. He actually stayed with my family for a short time after he was discharged and before he started college as a military veteran. We were just sixteen years apart in age and I had always been able to talk with him.

"Uncle Carl, I just had a lengthy conversation with a Vietnam vet, and I realized I have no idea what it's like to be in a war. You never talked about it very much when you came home, at least not with us kids. Didn't you say you were in charge of a prisoner of war camp?"

"No, not in charge; I was only a corporal. After I was in Fort Dix, New Jersey, I was twenty-two years old in 1944 when they loaded us on a converted destroyer to cross the Atlantic Ocean. It was right after the invasion of Normandy and D Day, and everything was in a state of confusion. We got to France twenty days later at ten o'clock on a moonlit night. There were no ports. The seas were choppy.

"The captain said, 'Johnny, you go first.' I had to climb down a rope to a raft made of barrels, which was pushed closer to shore by a small tug boat. We all jumped off into knee-deep water and waded into the shore and then to the top of a hill overlooking the beach. We saw German tankers abandoned on the shore. It was a fairly steep climb, but it wasn't actually a hill, because the land extending on inland was fairly flat. Almost immediately the hedgerows and small pasture-like fields were in front of us. Small fields were everywhere and all were enclosed, so to speak, by hedgerows instead of fences. It was in one of those fields we selected to camp for the night."

"So that was your first night in enemy territory?"

"Yes. That night I was posted as a guard on a road between two hedgerows about one hundred yards from our encampment with only my M-1 rifle. They expected guards to walk the road alongside the hedgerows in full view of any enemy on this moonlit night. Can you see anything wrong with that picture?"

"Yeah, you would be a sitting duck."

"Right. I found myself a spot alongside the hedgerow to partially conceal myself, still seeing up and down the road between the hedgerows. I got criticized for it, but I told them I was a better soldier alive than dead."

We laughed. I had always loved my uncle's sense of humor. He continued, "My most compelling dread was to have to shoot and possibly kill somebody. Would some drunken Frenchman understand orders like 'Halt, who goes there?' 'Advance and be recognized?' Or would he keep walking toward me? If anything seemed wrong, my orders were 'Shoot to kill.' Then, too, there was always the possibility of an enemy patrol into the so called liberated area of Normandy."

"Oh, that part of France was already liberated? So what were you doing there?"

"Okay, I'm finally getting to your original question. We were to build a prisoner-of-war camp, a POW camp. At first German POWs were all sent to England, but there were getting to be too many. The US Corps of Engineers came and put up two rows of high wire, making us a square prisoner-of-war camp with guard towers on opposite corners. They dubbed us Saint Low Prisoner of War Camp. Two hundred prisoners were herded in. Like I said, nothing was organized. We had to get them army pup tents to sleep in. I managed to get two big kettles set up for them to cook. From then on, I was the only American person to enter the POW camp, because I was the only American who spoke German. The food? Much of it was canned K-rations. I sent out a small detail of prisoners to get wood and water. The best thing I did was get them coffee. Potable water was a problem. At first we were furnished water in large containers. After that we made water safe to drink by using Lyster bags, which medicated the local water."

I couldn't believe how Uncle Carl was talking so freely. I decided the cost of the long distance minutes adding up didn't matter. This telephone conversation was priceless.

Uncle Carl continued, "The original prisoners were veteran soldiers. All we had to do was patch them up and check to make sure none had S.S. tattoos on their arms. The prisoners themselves would volunteer to help with work details. Everything went smoothly until rains came. We dug trenches to get rid of the water."

I asked, "Pup tents don't have any ground protection, right?"

"Right. It was cold and wet and miserable. I finally got smart. Up until then, I had been doing a lot of the work myself. That's when I identified the highest rank man—equivalent of first sergeant. From then on, I talked to him, and he dealt with the rest of the men."

This story was fascinating and I took notes as fast as I could.

Carl continued, "When we finished building this camp, they named me to help organize another POW camp. Remember, no one goes anywhere in a POW camp. We stayed put twenty-four hours a day, seven days a week. Otherwise, we were AWOL. There was one big difference in this second camp. We had some big tents. No one was on the ground. But there were still a lot of pup tents."

Carl took a long breath. "In the third POW camp, there were seven of us Americans in charge of one thousand German prisoners plus. It was near Chalons in eastern France. One section was a hospital. By then, the prisoners were mostly thirteen or fourteen years of age or very old German men. I still picked a German first sergeant to be in charge and that particular one came up with a lot of ideas. He called me, 'Herr Sergeant, these kids have so much energy, why not let them play soccer?' I brought the matter to the captain who approved, because he said he believed the war was winding down. Soccer teams and competitions were set up. It went over great. Next, the first sergeant spoke to me about artists in the group, so I found them paints and brushes in the Quartermaster's area, and they made actual paintings on boards. Last but not least, he told me about actors in the group. He asked if they could put on plays. That time I took two of them with me to see the captain in the front tent. The captain said yes and made some rules, such as nothing anti-American, nothing political. I got them wood, hammers, and saws, and they got busy building a stage. They put on a play full of crazy humor, silly episodes that had the soldiers doubling over with laughter, and it was a huge success."

"What happened to those POW camps?"

"After the war was over, they were turned over to the French. I was sent to Camp Lucky Strike where I waited and waited to be sent somewhere else. I wasn't sent to Japan though; I was sent back to the USA. So that was my war experience, my dear niece. Did I answer your question?"

"Yes, and then some. You know, one other thing I would like to know is what you feel now about your role in the war?"

"I worked hard. I set goals for the POWs. I organized them. I tried to keep them from escaping by telling them, 'Surely the war will be over soon and we will all go home. Let's all get home safely. Let's work together.' I knew it made sense to them when one night before the Battle of the Bulge quite a ways north of us, we were under attack by machine guns with a lot of hollering and shouting. In our tent, we dove to the floor and put out the pot belly stove. We were literally pinned down by machine gun fire and our tent was riddled with bullets. Our little stove exploded but we weren't hurt. In the morning we found that six prisoners broke out, but the rest refused to leave. It was a miracle that no one was hurt. But mainly it confirmed to me that the way we were treating the prisoners worked for everyone, considering the situation we were in."

"So you can say you were in combat."

"I was not a gung-ho-fight-for-liberty soldier. I would have been a very poor combat soldier. Fortunately a niche was available for me where I was able to do some good. At least, I like to think I did some good."

I was so grateful for Uncle Carl's honesty, and how he shared his practical, humane, and intelligent approach to serving in the army. It was peacemaking in the middle of war.

Uncle Carl was born in Iowa, but my dad came to the United States as a baby. Both of them and my Aunt Edith grew up speaking German. Surely their parents—my grandparents—had many moments of angst during the war, since all but one of their brothers and sisters and families lived in Germany. After the war, our family sent care packages regularly.

Everything on Memorial Day weekend started out as planned. EJ was going to marry Yoshiko Hirono, a Japanese airline stewardess with a college major in literature. EJ and Yoshiko planned to call the folks in Charles City, Iowa, after the civil ceremony. The time was to be two o'clock in the afternoon Central Standard Time. In order to be there for the call, Rachel, Markie, and I left Chicago very early that morning in my trusty Ford, which I dubbed "Tough

Buddy." We picked up our nineteen-year-old sister, Sydnee, in Iowa City on the way.

Sydnee was going to college, studying to be an elementary school teacher. We continued with no delay, calculating the time very closely to be at the home place when the long distance call came through. Sydnee asked if we knew how EJ and Yoshiko met. Rachel told the story.

"EJ was taking a train from southern Laos to Bangkok for one of his AID meetings, sitting by himself, reading a book. Across the aisle were four girls about his age, all talking at once in Japanese, laughing loudly. EJ thought they were acting very inappropriately from what he'd seen of other Asian females. He tried to ignore them. When they reached Bangkok, EJ happened to get in the customs-passport line behind the boisterous young ladies."

Sydnee said sarcastically, "Yeah, I'll bet our good-looking brother was in that line by accident."

Everyone laughed and Rachel went on with the story. "The girls continued with their flirting and silliness, and one of them switched to English and struck up a conversation with EJ. She told him they were all stewardesses on leave and three were going to meet boyfriends. Yoshiko was the exception, and for fun, the others had been eyeing EJ with the idea of matchmaking. One of the other girls suggested that EJ could join their group for some fun in Bangkok. That was how it all started."

Sydnee mentioned getting impatient with my driving. I hate to pass cars on two-lane highways. The traffic was heavy, so I located myself in line behind the car ahead of me. She said she was not afraid to pass cars, so she would be the best driver to get us to the folks' house in time for the phone call. We stopped, changed places, and continued north on Highway 61.

Before too long, she went to pass the car in front of us. I was shocked to see a whole line of cars headed right at us. She tried to merge into the line of cars going north as we were going, but no one would let us in.

"Sydnee, take the shoulder!" I yelled. She did. The left front wheel went over the ridge on the side of the road. We went into the ditch without rolling over. There were no seatbelts back then, but we all ended up in our seats, Rachel clutching Markie. We all looked at each other, stunned and relieved that everyone was okay.

We were at the bottom of a big ditch, headed the same direction of our previous travel. Up on the highway, I saw people that had stopped their cars, gotten out, and were standing there staring at us.

I hollered up at them, "Could someone call the police or get someone to help us?"

I heard someone say, "They must be on drugs. Let's get outta here."

The people looked at us as if we were from another planet. No one offered to help. They gradually drove off, leaving us by ourselves.

Sydnee said she would see if the car could still be driven. It started, but it wouldn't move. So much for getting there for the international phone call from EJ. I knew we had missed it. But at least we were still alive and unhurt.

I got out and walked up the ditch to the highway and saw a farmhouse across the highway. I kept going and knocked on the door. The woman who opened the door seemed puzzled, but said she would call a tow truck. A tow truck arrived within the hour. He said the front axle was bent. It would take a day to straighten it out and check over the car.

Sydnee called her fiancé, John, to come and pick us up. He listened to the story of what happened, and declared that Sydnee should have stayed in the passing lane. He said the guy coming toward us would have taken the side of the road, and then some-one would have let us in the lane of our direction of traffic.

Sydnee said, "Yeah, but it's Bev's car. In that split second who can analyze that way? I just did what Bev said to do."

"I'm glad you did, Sydnee." I opened my arms, really feeling thankful. "Hey, look at us. We're all alive and no one's hurt."

John repeated his assertion, this time telling me I was wrong.

I wasn't comfortable contradicting him, just felt strongly that I was right. "John, let's just agree to disagree. We were in their right-of-way. We were in the wrong. So we needed to make the correc-tion. A car is just a car. It can be replaced. Sydnee can't. Rachel can't. Markie can't. And I can't!"

That night we had dinner at John's parents' place. They invited us to stay overnight while we waited for my car.

Later that evening we were talking and John's dad asked me, "How do you pronounce Viet Nam? Is it pronounced *Nahm*? Or *Naam*?"

"I don't know for sure, but it seems to me that people who are against the war pronounce it *Nahm*. Those who believe we should be at war over there pronounce it *Naam*."

"What exactly is EJ doing in Vietnam?"

We three sisters pooled our knowledge. "Well, he's in Laos, not Vietnam. He's working for US AID which stands for United States Agency for International Development. EJ got the commu-nity working together to apply new water harvesting techniques from mountain streams to create a year-round irrigation system. He also introduced new rice types, so they could choose drought-resistant seeds. In doing all this, three villages are going from sub-sistence farming to making a cash crop of rice. He also introduced chickens. US AID built a local park, school building, and health clinic to serve families in the surrounding villages."

"Does he work mostly with small scale farmers?"

"Yes. EJ says he intends to keep in touch with the Laotian people he works with. He says they are friends for life."

Mildred, John's mother said, "What a difference one young guy straight out of college is making in the lives of all those families. We're studying the Beatitudes in church this summer. I think EJ is surely one of the blessed. Jesus said, 'Blessed are the peacemakers, for they will be called the children of God.'"

After we told them about some of the close calls EJ had experienced living so close to the Pathet Lao, John's father said, "Well, there're a lot of casualties of war over there, but what would you call it, God forbid, if EJ had been killed? Would he be a casualty of peacemaking?"

CHAPTER 8
No Summer Vacation

SUMMER, 1969

Even though I was thinking I could use a vacation at the beginning of the summer instead of at the end, because I was tired, I accepted my department chair's invitation to teach a summer school sewing class for adults. I had taught classes just like that when I was a full-time student in graduate school, and I thought it would be an easy way to make needed money. It was only a half day for four weeks, and it went well, even though I felt I was doing the work half-heartedly.

In the afternoons, I immersed myself in reading books on New Testament Thought and Historical-Critical Problems, taking notes, and taking notes to answer the questions for the written comprehensive exam requirement for my Master's Degree. I discovered something about myself—it was harder for me to finish a big project than to start it. At least I had a car now, so it was easier than taking the train to Northwestern/Garrett Library to check out books and other resources for addressing the questions. I drove to Evanston along Lake Shore Drive, which was always a feast for my eyes; Lake Michigan appeared different every time I went, sometimes gray and angry; sometimes blue and shiny. Timing-wise, I knew I needed to get the written exam turned in that summer and request to take the oral exam, so I could get my Master's Degree next spring; if not, my university study experience would be more than two years behind me. Never-the-less, I took time out and went to the beach to sunbathe on my way back from Evanston as often as I could. In July, I finally sat down to my manual typewriter and put my answers on paper. On July 18, 1969, I turned in my fourteen page written exam addressed to the three professors who would be my oral exam committee: Dr. Ernest Saunders, Dr. Al Sundberg, and a Dr. Perry. I signed off with a note to them:

> *I hope the readers have not had too much trouble reading through the typographical errors. I thank you profoundly for the time you have spent reading this and hope you found it a little bit enjoyable. In retrospect, I know it was a good experience for me.*

> *Signed, Beverly Johnson*

I was still trying to get up the courage to tell John that our dating relationship was all over and to mean it. He wouldn't call me for weeks on end, and then all of the sudden, I would get a call in which he was all bubbly and lovey-dovey, as I called it. I shared some of my embarrassment at being stood up so much with my roommates, and one day Rachel asked to have a serious sister-to-sister talk with me. She told me how much good her counseling was doing her, and she diagnosed me as being depressed and in desperate need of counseling myself. I had put her off the other times she made this suggestion, but I also remembered a personality test I took in graduate school after which the feedback recommendation was that I should consider counseling "if I wanted to be a happier person." I found myself considering seriously these scary ideas I had put off even thinking about for so long.

I tearfully wrote a final letter to John one Saturday night, which I never sent, but re-reading it several times finally gave me the courage to call a counselor. I made an appointment with a counselor recommended by my pastor. The letter which I recorded in my journal went like this:

My dearest Johnny,

The reason I'm writing this letter is that I wanted to get down in writing how you made a difference in my life. I can see that in the future, we shall be acting pretty mean to each other in many ways, and yet and still, underneath all of this, I know we have cared for each other. That caring has kept us seeing each other for two years, but I guess we've reached a point where it won't any longer. Anyway, here goes:

What I'm most thankful for is that we have trusted each other enough to share so much with each other. I've never been this open with a man before, but now I believe I can do it again if the right person comes along.

I guess I could never understand the kids at Waller nearly as well as I do, if I hadn't known you. You have changed my attitudes on many things such as how to have fun and how to love life and many more things.

Fun times we've spent together—at least for me—they are memories no one shall take away from me.

You were the one who convinced me to become a teacher instead of a dietitian. You were so right. I love it and I'm really good at it. Somehow you knew me well enough to know this about me.

You taught me how to dance.

So, John, no matter how many terrible things you do from

now on to hurt me, you can't take away those five good things. And no matter how many mean things I say to you from now on, you will always know I did love you and admired you, but now I declare my independence.

As I said, I never sent it. John always said I was the only girl he ever knew that wrote everything down. Even though I probably never sent him a letter, writing them out helped me clarify my thoughts and intentions, but this time it wasn't enough. I needed someone knowledgeable and objective from the outside with whom to share all this in order to understand myself better.

After getting acquainted, I began counseling with Mister Henry Cofer who assigned me to read the book *Games People Play* by Eric Berne. He said we would spend the next several counseling sessions applying those concepts to my life. I found it fascinating to read about human relationships by analyzing them as Parent-Adult-Child. After a few meetings with Mister Cofer, I recorded my first insights in my journal:

My Parent is mean, impersonal, relentless, punishing. My Adult is healthy, thinks things through, but gets pushed aside frequently by my Parent. My Child is healthy—it likes to have fun. Sometimes it is rebellious and then it also pushes my Adult aside. Also my Child brings out my Parent to punish itself for having fun. I need to develop a healthy Parent and a stronger Adult who can communicate with an Adult rather than a Child. My one most unhealthy Parent-Child relationship is with John. It consists of much giving on my part and little correspondence. I must bring to a conscious level what interactions are going on between him and me. Only then can I correct them.

He suggested I write down some of my interactions that next

week and then we could analyze them as Parent-Adult-Child. Here are two examples:

Bev: You said you were going to call me last night. (adult)

John: Gee, I forgot I said that. (child)

Bev: Why can't you remember your promises? (parent)

John: I was busy. I had things on my mind. (child)

And

John: I need some money. (child)

Bev: I'm not working right now. I don't have any to spare. (adult)

John: But it's a matter of life and death. (child)

Bev: Well, okay. You can have all I have on me. Pay me back. (parent)

John: Hell, yes. (child)

In both incidences when my Parent pushed my Adult aside, I was left feeling upset and even bitter. Then on top of that, my Parent reminded me of what I was always taught as a child—*it is improper to become angry; you children are so fortunate to have brothers and sisters; you should be kind to each other at all times.* I could see I was in a "catch-22" from which I really wanted to extricate myself, no matter how hard it was going to be.

My sister, Rachel, started divorce proceedings, which involved trips out to Denver where she and her husband lived. When their waiting period began, she decided to spend the summer in Chicago, then found a good steady babysitter for her toddler son, Markie. My church recommended a Humboldt Park neighborhood babysitter couple. Nieves (Mamita) and Daniel (Papito) Bajac were refugees from Cuba, because when Fidel Castro took over, Papito lost his government job and the new government confiscated their house. They left Cuba with practically nothing and came to stay in Chicago where they had relatives. They spoke Spanish, so Markie started learning to talk in two languages. He would grow up bilingual. Mamita and Papito's love for Markie expanded to include my sister, Rachel, and me, Markie's aunt. We all became part of their extended family and basked in genuine Latino hospitality.

What helped get me through my summer job and studying for the comps was my anticipation of a trip out west to visit Helen, my former work colleague in Mexico. She was married by then and lived in Salt Lake City. She planned to take me to go visit her parents in Butte, Montana, and go rafting. To get from Chicago to Salt Lake City, I took the train; it was my favorite way to travel. However, I discovered on the way that my wrists were becoming so painful I couldn't find a comfortable position. I bent my wrists and held my hands up, and I sat painfully still looking at the geography change as we crossed the Midwest and arrived at the mountains of Colorado and Wyoming.

My friend, Helen, was a nurse, and she was immediately alarmed about my painful wrists and my report that the pain was spreading to my knees and ankles. She knew I had rheumatic fever as a child, and she said that she wanted me to see her doctor before we left for Montana. We couldn't get an appointment until after that trip, so we left by car. I was starting to feel so fatigued from the pain that would not go away that I chose to ride in the car with Helen's parents instead of white water rafting. We watched Helen and her husband, and I felt like I did when I was a kid with rheumatic fever, sitting in the house watching my brother and sister play on the new swing set the folks bought for us to give me incentive to get better. I tried to make a joke out of my condition, telling

Helen's family what I always said when something unforeseen and negative happened, "This is a revolting development!" Her family laughed, but said they were worried about me.

Her doctor examined me, diagnosed rheumatic fever, and wanted to put me in the hospital. I said no, I needed to go back to Chicago. Although I hadn't seen a doctor since I was a full-time student, once I was back in Chicago, I promised I would look for a neighborhood doctor. If I couldn't find one, I would call Michael Reese Hospital where I used to work and ask for a recommendation. If I couldn't afford to pay for the appointment, I would wait until I started work again in September. I remembered that one of the things the teachers were asking for in the teacher strike was that the Board of Education offer health insurance to its employees. That was not approved, but the Chicago Teachers' Union intended to keep asking for it in future years. That seemed to be the new benefit that other companies were offering with employment. I was confident everything would work out for me. It always did.

On August 13 I wrote in my journal:

Tonight as I was talking on the phone with my new friend Julio I told him it isn't that easy finding a doctor. He suggested that maybe what I really need is a retiro espiritual. I have been going in circles all summer—working, studying for comps, babysitting, listening to my sister's problems, trying to go out as much as I can, reading my counseling assignments, sewing, cleaning. Even the visit with Helen failed to be relaxing. Maybe this swollen leg is another danger sign. Maybe all the rest of the summer should be of rest, decision-making, prayer, sun-bathing on the beach. The excuse for going nowhere is my leg. No one except Janice and Rachel needs to know I am here.

AUGUST 15-18, 1969

Farmer Max Yasgur saw it as a "victory of peace and love." Someone else described it as "one of the biggest rock festivals of all time and a cultural touchstone for the late sixties." What was it?

"The Woodstock Music and Art Fair: An Aquarian Exposition: Three Days of Peace and Music" was going to be the gathering of the century. It was more commonly known as the Woodstock Music Festival. Everyone wanted to go, but most of us couldn't go—mostly for lack of money, but I had another reason, too. Something was wrong with my health, although I didn't really think it was rheumatic fever—that was a child's disease. As it turned out, I would have needed robust health to survive the crush of a half-million young people gathered together on a dairy farm in the Catskills by Lake Erie in upstate New York.

Oh, the musicians that were rumored to be there! Credence Clearwater Revival was said to have been the first big name band to sign up. Also expected were Jimi Hendrix, Grateful Dead, The Who, Sha Na Na, Sly and the Family Stone, and Jefferson Airplane. Maybe we were not the first generation to do this, but we listened to our favorite singers' hits so many times, "we grooved on the beat," and we knew the words by heart.

In all there were thirty-two acts, including Joan Baez (who was six months pregnant) and Janis Joplin (who later died of a drug overdose.) I would have loved to see them and also Santana and his brass band. The weather was hot and steamy, but I guess no one noticed because of the quality performers and "Puff, the Magic Dragon." Of course there would be a lot of pot smoking at Woodstock. Someone always brought marijuana to share at concerts and parties in those days.

Julio called again and invited me to a "hippie party" for Chicago-based persons who couldn't go to Woodstock. I wore my favorite pair of red platform heels, bell bottom jeans, and a tie-dyed blouse I sewed myself. I knew clothing and hair styles were two big identifiers of our nonconformist generation. Another would be pot smoking.

I was trying not to be a prude. My date and I joined the partygoers sitting on pillows scattered around the main room of someone's apartment or lying on the floor rugs, listening to folk music. When the joint was passed around, I did like everyone else—take a drag, exhale with dramatic pleasure, say "good stuff," even though I felt nothing, and pass it onto the next person. Eventually we were supposed to "catch a high." I called it a "dry high," as contrasted with a similar feeling from drinking gin and tonic or another mixed drink.

Some of us were invited up to the second floor of the house for some "super good stuff." I went up, because it seemed to be the thing to do. A guy started the joint around, warning us not to take more than one drag. We passed it around. I didn't feel anything until I stood up to leave the room. Everything turned gray, then I was surrounded by stars. I pushed myself like a ton of bricks to the curved stairway. Halfway down I could go no further; I sat down on the step, put my head on my knees, and passed out. I have no idea how long I sat there that way. When I came to, many others were sitting down on the steps the same as me. I still felt foggy, but I got up, went to the kitchen, found some cold *mostaccioli* to eat, and drank a cup of black coffee.

That was the last time I smoked pot. What was there to enjoy about that experience? I was told the marijuana had been "laced" with something else—who knows what? Speed? LSD? Rat poison? I decided I couldn't trust the joints wrapped by—who knows who? When something is prepared or sold outside the law, mixed in someone's kitchen, there is no control whatsoever over the ingredients.

✻

On Labor Day weekend I got a surprise call from Clara, John's sister, who told me she was very, very sad that I was breaking up with her brother. She invited me and my roommates to an impromptu family picnic in Jackson Park "for old time's sake." She said she had all the food ready, just bring ourselves. John, their uncle, and her husband, Frazier, would be there.

We met by the Museum of Science and Industry and walked east and south past the German submarine that was captured during World War II. We walked until we found a place under a shade tree with a view of Lake Michigan to spread out a tablecloth and open the picnic baskets. John was talking incessantly about looking at a house to buy near Pill Hill on the South Side. After eating and enjoying the wonderful warm weather, the guys went off somewhere for a walk.

We four gals cleaned up and sat down on the cloth in a circle to talk while we enjoyed our glasses of ice cold lemonade. Markie went to sleep, as Clara was telling us about their sister Josie's wedding in Biloxi, Mississippi, their hometown. All of a sudden, she burst out in tears. Anxiously we asked her, "What's wrong? What is it?" She just kept crying, shaking her head. Rachel asked, "Aren't you feeling well?"

Between sobs, she said, "We never had a picnic like this when I was growing up in Biloxi. We couldn't even be on the same beach with white folks."

I asked, "What didya do, Clara?"

"Me and my brother and sisters walked around the white peoples' beaches all the way to the end to our beach. When I was little, I always wondered why it was that way."

I offered, "I guess those days are behind us."

Clara responded, "Oh, my god, I wish they were."

I thought better of my overly optimistic assessment. "I'm sorry, Clara, I'm wrong a lot lately. Did I ever tell you that my college roommate, Anna Mae, and I went to hear Martin Luther King when he came to Chicago to march in Cicero?"

"I remember he wanted to march in that all-white suburb, but somehow the march was prevented there. They had to march somewhere else."

"Yeah, Doctor King really looked beaten down and extremely disappointed on the stage that night."

"What did he say about that?"

"I wish I could get ahold of the text, but I do remember he said, 'I'm tired of marching for something that should have been mine at birth. I'm tired of living every day under the threat of death. I'm tired of all of the surging murmur of life's restless sea.' "

"You have such a good memory, Bev."

"Well, how could anybody forget MLK?"

"What a loss. What a loss to us all."

Rachel asked, "Bev, didn't Anna Mae marry a black guy?"

"Yes, Ivan is Latino, born in Jamaica and grew up in Panama. I was Anna Mae's maid of honor. I always admired her. She was brilliant—he was, too, and they were so comfortable talking about everything including race."

When we were saying our good-byes, Clara took me aside and told me that her brother's girlfriend was going to move in with him after he bought the house. She was sending for her kids. She said that place will probably be in a constant uproar. With her arm around my shoulders, she said even more sadly, "Sorry you and Johnny couldn't make it. I wish you could've helped him grow up, but thankfully he's finally becoming a man." At that moment I was sadder about never seeing Clara again than I was about losing Johnny.

CHAPTER 9
A Major Setback or Two

FALL, 1969

I myself became a living casualty of peacemaking at the beginning of my second year of teaching. I learned the hard way that even an energetic thirty-year-old cannot work and keep going beyond her physical limits. I reported to Waller High School for my second year of teaching with painful joints and intense fatigue. I taught my first three classes, then skipped lunch and collapsed on the couch in the teachers' washroom. I simply could not force myself to get up again. My teacher colleagues covered my afternoon classes. I reported to work again the next day. The same thing happened.

My department head insisted I see a doctor and she recommended a local one. I started to use my sick days. After the doctor diagnosed and treated me for rheumatoid arthritis, I was feeling worse instead of better. I called Michael Reese Hospital where I used to work to hopefully get a more trustworthy medical doctor. The new doctor said it was highly unusual, but reluctantly confirmed the diagnosis, a recurrence of my childhood rheumatic fever. He was concerned how much weight I lost, and that my weight of only 130 pounds at 5'7 ¾" was too low for my body structure. Since heart infection could cause permanent heart damage which was life-threatening, he ordered me to take a leave of absence from work.

His other orders were complete bed rest, prescription-amounts of aspirin taken with ice cream (to protect my stomach) every four hours day and night to keep my body temperature down, and to come in to see him twice a month. The point was to prevent any further heart damage while my body healed.

Wondering how I got this disease again, I knew it had to be different from the first time when I was five or six years old. That time my body had been cold a lot. My father would walk with me to the nearest country school one mile from our farm home holding my hand or carrying me on his shoulders if there was too much snow. Winters were cold in northern Iowa and I would sit in the cold one-room school house, shivering and waiting for the teacher to get there. Then I went down to the basement with her while she shoveled coal in the furnace and started the fire burning. Finally, the school heated up. My first bout of rheumatic fever started with what was once called Saint Vitus Dance, a temporary loss of small and large muscle control. My second bout at age thirty started over the summer with extremely painful wrists, knees and ankle joints that gradually worsened to debilitating fatigue.

Rheumatic fever is an inflammation of the heart caused by the streptococcus bacterium. I didn't remember having strep throat, but the doctor said it could have been a low grade throat infection. We figured out I was probably infected the past year during dental work (no mouths covered with masks back then.) I did remember the dentist coughing and sneezing one or two times, and me wishing he would turn his head and not blow germs so near my mouth. The only way to knock out a bacterial infection was by an antibiotic shot, which my current doctor administered. He prescribed monthly preventative penicillin shots thereafter. Since there was no health insurance back then, or at least not for teachers, he said he would refer me to the Chicago Board of Health for monthly shots.

Having to be off work for at least two months, I soon realized the leave of absence actually was a gift of time. For the last year and a half, I had been in a whirlwind of work, study, and activity. During my first year of teaching, I went to new teacher workshops almost every Saturday to improve my teaching. Every Sunday I played the organ for two church services—one in Spanish and one in English. I was constantly on the go, even all summer when I was supposedly on vacation. While I taught summer school, I studied and turned in my written comprehensive exams for my Masters of Art degree, as well as starting to prepare for defending them whenever they called me in for the oral exam. I did fun things, too—for instance, I went to Cubs baseball games every Tuesday they were home, because Tuesday was "Ladies Day." Free for me.

Now all of a sudden, there was really nothing but empty time and forced inactivity. It was as though my worn-down body was saying to me: *This is your body speaking now. My dear, you have been running at maximum speed and intensity for too long. You became exhausted and didn't seem to know it. You need to rest and recuperate, thank you.*

A sad part of being sick was that I completely lost track of most of my so-called friends. I was disappointed, but had to face the reality that everyone was carrying on with their own lives and doing their own thing. I was grateful for my two roommates, Janice and Rachel, who insisted it was no extra trouble letting me camp out on the living room sofa during the day and eat supper with them for which they cooked, shopped, and cleaned. They both stuck by me through what turned into a leave of absence of three long months—they never once complained.

I got to catch up on recreational reading. One magazine article which I re-read many times helped me feel better about the lost friendships. It said there are different types of friendship and there are three kinds of friends:

1. *Go-Go Friends* enjoy the same kinds of activities and like to do those activities together with you.

2. *Short-Term Friends* are meaningful to you, because you meet each other's needs during a certain time period in your life span.

3. *Best Friends* are those with whom you feel empathy and a closeness that grows and changes as the two of you grow and change. They accept you when you are down and out, as well as when life is bright and sunny. This third type of friend is rare and we don't have many best friends in our lifetimes, but I knew Janice and Rachel were my best friends.

My fellow Peace Corps teachers were *short-term friends*. I could imagine them continuing to help make this a more peaceable world. I heard that Maurice followed his dream, went overseas to Africa, and formed a new love relationship that he said was going to lead to marriage. Carlos, being born in Puerto Rico, discovered he didn't know much about his people or his homeland when he visited his aunt and uncle after he graduated from high school. He was learning when he taught art and culture in the summer program, and as an activist, by now was surely pouring his time and energy and creativity in his studies to become a middle school teacher in Chicago.

Bruce's work as a young pastor with the Young Lords gang was causing waves in the community, as it was impacting the lives of the leaders of the gang. They were probably absorbing his passion for social justice, exchanging their random violence for positive albeit radical actions to help their Latino brothers and sisters raise themselves out of poverty. They provided a day care center in the church, so the local women could work and they convinced the city to replace nearby substandard housing with new subsidized apartment living.

My brother, EJ, said he formed lasting friendships with the people of the villages of Laos in which he worked, similar to what I did with the people in Chihuahua, Mexico, when I was in the short-term mission program. Most importantly, he was married now and was going to bring his new bride, Yoshiko, home to Iowa with him very soon, right around Thanksgiving. I told myself that I had to get better by then, so I could meet them at the Chicago airport and we could all drive together to a grand homecoming in Iowa. That was barely two months away, so getting my health back became my grand goal and motivated me to follow doctor's orders even when I didn't want so much bed rest.

Rachel decided to stay in Chicago on her teaching job. I really bonded with my little nephew, Markie, who was in those "terrible twos." He was very active and would run and get things for me while I babysat. He played by himself, and we read children's books together. His favorite book was *Great Grandpa Bunny Bunny.* He loved that the rabbit great-grandpa taught the rabbit grandchildren how to color Easter eggs and that they knew it was their great-grandpa who colored the rainbows and beautiful sunsets after he died. Maybe Mark liked it because his father had disappeared from his life.

My mother became my telephone pal. Since long distance calls to Iowa cost quite a bit per minute back then and Mom knew my money was short, she called me once a week. She said it was important for me to keep my spirits up and she was going to help me do so. I found I enjoyed talking with her on a whole range of subjects. Once she surprised me saying she felt guilty about my getting rheumatic fever in the first place. She said that if she had just figured out before I started school that the boundary roads of our rural township indicated that I actually should have been going to town school, not country school, then I could have ridden a school bus to town school that first year and I might never have gotten sick. She said she didn't investigate it thoroughly, because she was so happy I would be attending the same country school in which she had taught the years before she married Dad. When Mom spoke about her role in how I might have avoided rheumatic fever, I told her that seemed like a game of "What if?" and "Who knows?" I told Mom not to feel bad, because I was glad I had the country school experience, even if it was only one year. It made me feel like an authentic town-and-country girl.

I reminisced with Mom that after my cousin Cheryl and I finished our daily primary grade (now called kindergarten) lessons, we would sit quietly and listen to the teacher teach the first through eighth grade kids in the one room country school. I told Mom I must have learned a lot in country school, because my first grade teacher, Miss Priebe, in McKinley Elementary School in Charles City, always introduced new concepts in reading and arithmetic by asking who already knew. I would always raise my hand. She effectively cut me off by asking in an irritated voice, "Does anyone besides Beverly know the answer?"

My relationship with my mother was changing. I was still trying to keep the peace by avoiding any controversy, but because of counseling, I now recognized when I was playing the child role, trying to gain her approval. I tried to express my opinions as an adult and share my feelings more honestly with her. In return, I noticed she pretty much quit being moralistic and giving parental advice. I would say our relationship was in the process of changing from a predominantly parent-child interaction to more of an adult-adult interaction.

✴

To make the best of a bad situation, my friends from the Humboldt Park Spanish congregation and Pastor Guillermo Debrot told me I needed a television set to watch while I was to lay flat on my back. I told them I didn't need one, because I never watched television. However one day the pastor and a parishioner simply paid me a surprise visit with a used seventeen-inch black and white television set in hand and insisted on connecting it in our living room, including an aerial called "rabbit ears" for reception.

I discovered I thoroughly enjoyed *M*A*S*H* (comedy hospital team series during the Korean conflict), *Perry Mason* (trial lawyer series), *Columbo* (private investigator/detective series), *American Bandstand with Dick Clark* (popular music with youth dancing rock and roll), *I Love Lucy* (comedy marriage series with Lucille Ball and Desi Arnaz), and *The Ed Sullivan Show* (variety show with famous entertainers), and more. Two nightly news broadcasts. Walter Cronkite and *The Huntley and Brinkley Report* made the news interesting with thoughtful commentaries and the *Saturday Night Live* spoof of the news was hilarious.

No longer in the "rat race" of work and activities, I had my first chance to unhurriedly reflect on the last year and a half. I don't think I could have written this book many years later without having a lengthy time to remember and reflect.

Then one day everything changed.

September 30, 1969—*Chicago Tribune* headline:

North Side Cleric, Wife Slain: Couple Found Stabbed in their Home
Minister Aided Street Gangs

A wave of dread passed over me as I picked up the morning paper that lay outside our apartment door. The headline jarred me in the gut and my intuition told me this was someone I knew.

"Oh, dear God, it can't be."

My worst fears were confirmed when I unfolded the paper enough to see the picture of Reverend Bruce Johnson, my friend, the pastor who was full of life directing Mayor Daley's Peace Corps Program in the Armitage Avenue Methodist Church just a little more than one year ago. I rushed into the kitchen to share the devastating news with my sister, Rachel, and roommate, Janice.

I was near tears. "It's horrible. You'll never believe who's in the paper, sis." I dropped into a chair near the table where the two of them were having coffee. My eyes filled with tears. Nausea swept over me and my voice cracked as I tried to read the article aloud between sobs. Rachel grabbed the paper from me and read the front page article to us, "Police questioned friends, neighbors, and parishioners of a north side Methodist minister last night in the search for clues to the killer of the minister and his wife in their apartment at 2038 Seminary Avenue. Former parishioners of the church, whose regular membership reportedly had dwindled to less than a dozen, also were to be questioned about the murder of the Rev. Bruce W. Johnson, 30, and Marjorie Eugenia Johnson, 31."

Rachel stopped. "How could anyone do such a thing? Oh, oh, oh, how awful. I can't read any more."

Janice took the paper and scanned the rest of the story, "Bruce and Eugenia were murdered late Sunday night. The mailman found one of their little twins sitting on the front steps crying, covered with blood stains. The front door was wide open. The mailman looked inside and found the minister slumped in his rocking chair—dead from multiple stab wounds. He heard crying, went to the bedroom to investigate, and found the other twin crying in a crib. Eugenia was lying dead on the floor in a bedroom. The twins were not hurt. He called the police."

Janice interrupted herself, "I can't believe what I'm reading. What kind of a person would murder a minister and his wife, especially with their two little children right there! And just leave them? Imagine, not even being safe in your own home!"

I couldn't believe what Rachel and Janice had read. I sat there shaking my head from side to side. "Do they know who did it? Did they find the killer?"

"No. It says police are investigating. Let's see. Robbery might have been the motive, because they found his wallet thrown on the floor with the money missing. Police assume Johnson knew the killer, because there were no signs of breaking in and there were two coffee cups on the table."

Tears streaming down her cheeks, Rachel spoke with shaking voice, "Doesn't it say the minister was known for working with street gangs? Oh, poor Bruce and Eugenia. She was so sweet and quiet. He was so passionate about reaching out to inner city youth. It had to be a street gang member! They were always hanging around the edges of our summer program. Remember, sis? Bruce wouldn't let anyone in our program who belonged to a gang. I hate gangs!"

I grabbed a napkin and wiped away my tears. "I suppose police think it's a gang member, too, because money was stolen. But you know what? It could be a frame-up. Bruce was a very controversial character. Didn't the paper say they were questioning former church members? There may have been other people who had motives for killing him."

Janice stood up with her hands on her hips and glared at me. "No, I don't believe that for a minute. I've worked in enough churches to know that members can get really mad at a pastor, but usually they up and leave the church. You are all wrong to accuse his church members!" She walked over to the window and looked out.

I felt as if she had slapped me, but I said to her back, "Janice, I'm not accusing them, but there were parishioners that summer who made a really big deal over Carlos and his class painting Puerto Rican art on the basement walls. Rachel and I remember how one guy confronted Carlos when he was finishing painting the stairway walls that last day. They weren't quite done with the stairs, but he told him his summer job was over."

"Yeah, that guy was angry for some reason, but I agree with Janice, that's not something to kill over," Rachel said.

"That's probably true," I conceded. "I found out that after the Second World War, the Armitage church members went way out on a limb to sponsor jobs for Japanese Americans so they could get out of the concentration—relocation—camps. That church has always believed in working for justice. We worked there that summer because the church members approved the summer youth program to keep Puerto Rican kids off the streets and in school."

Janice sat down again and lowered her head like she was praying. After a moment of silence, I continued, "I just got the impression the current church membership didn't believe Bruce should have been working with the Young Lords street gang. That gang might well have pushed their tolerance too far."

Rachel answered with a wavering voice, "Maybe it's a generational problem in the church. Bruce was quite young for a pastor, and the paper said the church membership had dwindled to less than a dozen. As I remember, they were all very old. Bruce really cared about youth. He used to say we have to give them hope and show them how to succeed in a city that doesn't give a hoot about them. That's what he liked Bev and me doing—getting kids involved in their own learning."

"And he used to say we were helping prepare leaders who could help their own people. Because gang leaders already had developed leadership skills, I remember hearing Bruce say they needed a goal and a change of heart to put their talents to productive use."

"They need more than a change of heart." Janice stood up again and walked around the room. "Can't you two see they're criminals? Bruce was very naive if he was trying to convert kids when human life doesn't mean anything to them. The paper said Bruce let the killer in—that he knew him. No church member would come calling that late at night. No. It had to be that gang—what were they called again?"

"Young Lords."

"What were those kids like?" she asked.

"Some were older than just kids," said Rachel.

"Yeah, all summer we heard talk about their leader, Cha-Cha Jimenez. Remember how the kids in the summer program respected him? Our buddy, Carlos, wasn't a gang member himself, but he respected Cha-Cha. The Young Lords were fighting something they called gentrification in Lincoln Park."

"Please tell me, what is gentrification?"

"To be honest, I'm not sure." Suddenly I put two and two together in my mind. "When I saw Carlos last spring, he was telling me how he worked with the Young Lords all last year. Of course, that's what they were doing—fighting against gentrification. Young professionals working in the Loop and living in the suburbs wanted to take over Lincoln Park with condominiums and ritzy apartment buildings, because it was an easier commute to jobs in the Loop. The Young Lords really took issue when the city tore down storefronts with second floor apartments on the corner of Armitage and Halsted, and in their place, they were going to put tennis courts on the lot. They put up a big hand-painted sign saying PEOPLE'S PARK to claim the empty lot for the people of the neighborhood."

Rachel banged her open hand on the table. "Don't try to make out like gangs are any good. They are bad news. Period."

"Actually I agree with you, Rachel." Janice pointed her finger at me. "You're wrong, Bev. See? When those gangs want something, they get it any way they can!"

"It sounds like a turf war over Lincoln Park," I said.

"Big stakes turf war. And Bruce Johnson was right in the middle of it!" Rachel said.

"I've got to think about that," I said. "Might there be another motive for killing the Johnsons?"

Janice picked up the empty coffee cups and took them to the sink for washing. I stopped talking to give all three of us a chance to cool off. I started to think about the possible effects Reverend Johnson had on the neighborhood, the church community, and the city. Surely Mayor Daley would have been happy with how the summer program kept kids off the streets. After all, the city was hosting the 1968 Democratic convention and the city fathers wanted to make a good impression on the world. Would the mayor have predicted that the "Power to the People" slogan would go as far as the Young Lords took it? I broke the silence.

"Gee whiz. I feel like a detective on TV trying to solve a convoluted murder mystery. Do you think some politician or big wig real estate tycoon could've hired a stupid druggie or gang member to kill Bruce? Then his wife got killed, too, because she recognized the killer? Like you yourself said, Janice, some people don't seem to care about a human life."

Janice covered her ears, "Stop! I can't stand this talk anymore. Let's stop it right now."

"Okay, I'll stop. I'm sorry, Janice, I'm sorry, Rachel."

I decided to call my pastor, Reverend Jim Neuman. I wanted to find out what he thought and I needed to talk to someone who might have a different point of view from my roommates. I went to the phone in the front room, lay down on my usual sofa, and dialed the number. No answer. I tried again, in case I dialed wrong. Finally I heard Ruth, Reverend Neuman's wife, answer, "Hello."

"Hi, Ruth. It's Bev. Did you hear about the Johnsons?"

"Yes, isn't it awful about them being killed?"

"I still can't believe it. Do you think it was some gang member?"

"I suppose it was. Maybe it was a drug addict. They went through his wallet for money."

"It's so sad. How long did you know him?"

"We met Bruce and Eugenia when Jim was appointed to Humboldt Park. There was a Methodist church and an Evangelical United Brethren church located within blocks of each other. After our two churches merged, Bruce got appointed to the Armitage Avenue Methodist Church. I knew he had a youth ministry in Lincoln Park like he had when he was in Humboldt Park."

I asked, "Are you going to the funeral?"

"I wish I could." A heavy sigh came through the receiver. "But the funeral's gonna to be Friday night in Rockford; that's more than 100 miles away from Chicago. Both Bruce and Eugenia's parents live in Rockford. Can you imagine what they're going through? They must be heartbroken. I especially feel bad about Eugenia and the children. She did absolutely nothing to bring such evil upon them."

"You mean to say the parishioners aren't doing anything in Chicago?"

"I heard there'll be a community memorial service at the Armitage Church."

"When?"

"Tomorrow night."

I thanked her for the information and we said we would see each other soon when I could get back to church.

I felt I had to go to the memorial service, even though I wasn't supposed to go anywhere. I didn't drive, because I figured there would be no parking places. Rachel and I got off the bus at the corner of Armitage and Halsted. The empty lot, still designated as People's Park, was filled with hundreds of people—all ages, all races and nationalities. There were people with guitars, priests, community residents. It was getting dark. I searched the crowd for Carlos, but I didn't see anyone I knew.

Rachel spoke in a lowered voice, "Just like that summer. This is another coming together of the races and nationalities. Isn't this something?"

"It's overwhelming," I whispered back. "I wish Bruce could've had such a big crowd of people coming to hear him preach while he was alive."

Just then a loudspeaker crackled and blared: "Hello. I'm Robert Colon of the Comancheros. We're all here to give our respects to the Reverend Mister Bruce Johnson. He came to serve the community with an open heart and open mind. He wanted us to have a share in this neighborhood and everyone be proud of who we are. All he wanted was to make us happy. He wouldn't want this occasion to be a sad one. Come. Follow me to the church."

Guitars were strumming and the people singing in what I imagined to be the style of a New Orleans funeral march. Among the neighborhood people, I recognized the Young Lords with their black berets. I figured it was the Comancheros street gang wearing red berets. And there were young men dressed all in black who must have been from the Illinois Black Panthers Party.

Rachel said, "I can't believe all these street gang members are here. It looks like they're the ones who organized the memorial. I'm nervous. Let's go home, sis."

"No, I want to stay. We're already here. Maybe we'll get some of our questions about gangs answered. It seems they genuinely respected Bruce. They weren't just using him."

Reluctantly, Rachel agreed and we joined in the parade, walking down the city block to the church. It was a bit of a shock to see the big canvas hung over the front of the church with the words LINCOLN PARK PEOPLE'S CHURCH. Hundreds of people were standing around outside the church. Someone told us that the inside of the church was already full. There were some loudspeakers attached to the bell tower. We could hear the singing of hymns and spirituals.

"Rachel, you wait here. I'm going to go in the back stairway and see what things look like inside. I just have to see for myself. Then I'll come back. It sounds like we'll be able to hear everything okay out here, all right?"

Rachel nodded. "Come right back."

Multicolored balloons taped to the pews rose up in the church. At the altar there was a homemade cross with candles lit on either side. On the wall was a picture of a hangman's tree with a full moon in the background. THEY WERE MURDERED was printed underneath. There must have been three hundred people sitting in the pews and standing around the sanctuary. I quickly left to rejoin my sister outside. Speaker after speaker repeated that the pastor had not died in vain. They said Reverend Johnson did everything he could to build up the community, and now his task had become everyone's task. They pledged to continue his work and bring people together. A beautiful voice sang, "I was once was lost, but now I'm found."

Someone passed out candles to the crowd listening to the service outside. Tears were flowing everywhere. Nearby, voices were praying in Spanish and English along with the service. Most people looked stunned. A thousand people must have gathered outside the church before the service was over. I was sure Bruce and Eugenia didn't know they were loved by so many.

In the days to come, the Young Lords blamed the powers-to-be *that* for Bruce's death. They made a statement in the *Chicago Defender* newspaper:

> *These murders show to what vicious lengths some people will go to prevent the growth of a just struggle. Instead of attacking us the way others in his position might have done, Rev. Johnson, his wife, and the board of the church knew our demands were justified and supported us. They helped greatly in our efforts to open a free day care center [in the church basement], and helped tell others of our needs, and the correctness of our action.*

The Alderman George McCutcheon (43rd Precinct) blamed the Young Lords. He also blamed them for firebombing his office two weeks prior to the murders. He told the church board that they were being taken in by the Young Lords and that their day care center in the church basement was a front for their acts of violence in the community.

Government agencies that investigated the dual murders included the Chicago Police Department, the GIA (Gang Intelligence Unit), and the FBI, according to the newspapers. The murderer was never identified; no one was charged. The murders remained unsolved. As Ruth Neuman told me, "Jim thinks there are pieces missing and that the police know more than they disclosed. It's all very sad."

It became a cold case. Questions were left unanswered. I wished for a long time that someone would investigate it again and bring the murderer to justice.

My conclusion was that anyone who goes far above and beyond, as did Bruce Johnson, to give a legitimate voice to power-less people is entering a dangerous world. When there are multiple power holders, there's much at stake. There have to be winners and losers in the power struggle.

I couldn't help but remember all the murders and assassina-tions in 1968, especially Robert Kennedy and Martin Luther King, and of course President John Kennedy years before. I asked myself: *Why do all the good guys die? Was it because they were peacemakers who were speaking up for the youth, the poor, the minorities, and the powerless? Bruce wasn't a famous and well-known world leader, but to those community people who came out to pay their respects to him, he was just as important as any other martyr.*

In the next days, I cried whenever I thought about the deaths of Bruce and Eugenia. In my thirty years of life, I had not lost anyone to death except my two paternal grandparents. I hadn't seen or talked to the Reverend Bruce Johnson for over a year, but his death shook me up. He was my same age, and he had been so full of life the year before. Now he was dead.

I talked by phone to one of his former church members who was then in the Humboldt Park church, and learned that some young people didn't care for his brashness and controversial opin-ions, but I hadn't experienced that side of him. I admired him and his tragic death made no sense to me. It was doubly tragic that the murderer would kill his quiet devoted wife only because she prob-ably recognized the murderer. I kept imagining the bloody murder scene in my thoughts and dreams until I knew my fury toward the murderer, whoever it was, went beyond healthy anger. I wondered how a murderer could cover his tracks so well. I knew since the FBI and the Chicago Police Department couldn't solve the case, it would surely do me no good to fantasize that I could become an amateur detective and try to solve the murders. Columbo made it look easy, but I could do nothing about this grave injustice any more than I could solve the assassinations of John F. Kennedy and Martin Luther King, Jr.

I actually got tired of crying, and that was when I decided to try to consciously limit my own remembrances of Bruce to things positive. I spent hours remembering incidents during the summer school program. I wanted to remember Bruce for what he lived for, not what he died for. But I then realized that he died for what he lived for. He lived to save angry young people from violent lives in gang activity and help them open up to a productive life for themselves. When his own life was threatened, he didn't fight back. The newspaper account said he was sitting upright in his chair when he died. He died with dignity. I decided to remake my permanent mind picture of Bruce into what he looked like to me that last day of summer school. His face was bright and hopeful, as he spoke passionately to us about what a difference we teachers had made in the lives of the neighborhood kids.

I decided I would try to adopt his leadership style of inspiring people and then allowing them the freedom to work out their own ideas, giving permission instead of criticism, empowering young people to think for themselves and take action on their ideas. The more difficult part of his personality to emulate was his nonviolence even in the face of death. Maybe he was in denial of reality, but maybe he was truly Christ-like in how he faced his murderer. To try to understand, I turned to that enigmatic author Dietrich Bonhoeffer, who was also my age when he was jailed and executed in Nazi Germany. His writings were so deep, I could barely understand him, but somehow they made me feel better. In an Advent 1937 sermon entitled, "The Cost of Discipleship," he preached,

> *By willingly renouncing self-defense, Christians affirm their absolute adherence to Jesus, and their freedom from the tyranny of their own ego ... the only power which can overcome evil. Suffering willingly endured is stronger than evil; it spells death to evil.*

(Bonhoeffer, Dietrich, "A Testament to Freedom." New York: Harper One, 1980, page 317)

Indeed, after so many purely evil professional-type assassinations of important peacemakers in the 1960s, Bruce's murder could be counted as just one more. Contrary to breeding more evil, Bruce's nonviolence was energizing the Puerto Rican community and bringing people together.

On the eighth of October, I was again shocked by what I saw on the local Chicago news—mobs of antiwar young people running down the streets, throwing things at buses and stores, and breaking windows. Right away I guessed the perpetrators had to be some of those very demonstrators I remembered from the year before, the ones in Lincoln Park who wanted to "bring the war home."

Watching the repeated news versions and mob scenes dubbed, "The Days of Rage," I didn't think the violent demonstrators proved anything to anyone, and they certainly did not turn anyone against the Vietnam War. Rather, The Days of Rage took the public's minds away from the comparatively nonviolent antiwar demonstrations of the summer before, those which drew participation from thousands of college kids and young adults during the Democratic

147

Convention. The Illinois Black Panther party and the Students for a Democratic Society (SDS) denounced The Days of Rage.

Many people in the public came to confuse the two demonstrations—thinking the Days of Rage of October 8-11, 1969, were the same as the nondestructive demonstrations of the previous summer at the 1968 Democratic Convention. Both started in Lincoln Park, but this time, it was a faction of the SDS called the Weathermen who called for and carried out the mayhem and caused the property damage. Unfortunately, the county sheriff was injured. The Illinois National Guard was again called in to help the Chicago Police Department control the bouts of violence.

In spite of The Days of Rage, it seemed to me that television coverage of serious war resisters might be becoming more sympathetic. There was a feature story about a young man caught in the tug of war between breaking the law by leaving the country and complying with a "bad warrior law." The Vietnam War was becoming widely understood as one country's civil war, not the United States saving Southeast Asia from the powerful tide of Communism.

The American law for compulsory military service didn't seem to apply equally to all Americans like it did when it was enacted for the Second World War. Families with power and privilege such as senators and representatives may have had sons, but most were not serving in the military for one reason or another. Yet other draft resisters didn't have many options that were not illegal.

The government dealt ruthlessly with young men who failed to register for the draft at age 18 and with others given A-1 status, who were approved for active duty by their draft boards, but refused to report for military training. Mohammad Ali won the heavyweight boxing title in 1967, but was arrested, found guilty of draft evasion, forced to renounce his title, and was sent to jail. Others reported for training, went AWOL (away without leave), and were chased down until captured and sent to the "brig," a punishing military jail. Still others stayed in training camps, but refused to cooperate with the regimen, got court marshalled, and were given a dishonorable discharge. Draft age resisters could avoid the whole process only by leaving the country, escaping to Canada or Mexico where, as USA citizens, they lived illegally. Had they returned home before the war's end, they too would have discovered how illegal their actions were.

There were very few legal options for not going to war. Some like my brother, EJ, took the unpopular route of reporting to the draft board, declaring to be a conscientious objector, and doing "alternative service." I saw this as the only option that would earn one the label of peacemaker. Some eighteen-year-olds put off being drafted by going to college, graduate school, and even seminary. In my experience, I was amazed how many male students were up-front about their enrolling in a seminary to evade the draft. Although I empathized with their stand against the war, I felt that some professions such as the ministry or teaching required a calling; they were careers that needed stronger motivation and commitment than just wanting to avoid going to war. I wondered what kind of pastors and teachers they would become. Yet I figured I couldn't be judgmental, because it seemed so unfair for our country to force law-abiding, peace-loving young men into becoming criminals, escapees, or bitter disgruntled workers in important jobs for which they had no passion or calling. I knew exactly why I was against the draft.

President Lyndon Johnson had taken office when Kennedy was assassinated and he worked with Congress to accomplish miracles such as the Civil Rights Act after he was elected in his own right. Yet despite his campaign pledge not to widen military involvement in Vietnam, he soon announced that the draft would be doubled and voluntary enlistment programs would be intensified so that we could win that war. By 1967, American military strength went up to 525,000 troops fighting alongside 600,000 South Vietnamese troops. (Daugherty, Leo, *The Vietnam War Day by Day*. New York: Chartwell Books, Inc., 2002, page 54) Mounting protests against the war probably caused him not to run for the Democratic nomination in 1968. Perhaps he was caught between two implacable forces—the war-making military machine that said they needed many times the troops they already had in order to win the war, and the youthful peace movement, which Kennedy was believed to have supported, because he originated the Peace Corps. The candidate vacuum had been filled by vice president Hubert Humphrey, who lost the election to Richard Nixon.

It still bothered me that newspapers and television were not making much attempt to present the motivations of the war protesters. However, there was one time that war protesters actually had a voice that was heard throughout the media—during the Democratic Convention. But when the trial of the war protesters began, everyone's hopes were dashed. Of all things, Judge Hoffman prohibited any mention of the Vietnam War during trial testimony and questioning. He limited the trial to one question: was there was a conspiracy to create violence and disruption? Therefore the trial of demonstrators (primarily) and policemen (secondarily) during the Democratic Convention was dubbed the *Conspiracy Eight Trial*. I began to wonder if the real conspiracy was to bar the public from learning that even the most outrageous of the protest leaders were actually deeply committed to giving young people a voice regarding the interminable continuation of the Vietnam

War. Maybe the real conspiracy was against anyone making a good case against war.

Abby Hoffman and Jerry Rubin were the stars of the Conspiracy Eight show. William Kunstler, the lawyer I had met, and Leonard Weinglass, the other defense attorney, were the supporting actors. As defendants, they played to the television audiences, trying to solicit sympathy for their cause. But what was their cause? Since they couldn't try to sway the American public against the Vietnam War which was Plan A, they adopted Plan B—their antics seemed to be designed to reveal the warlike mentality of the police, the government prosecutors, and Judge Julius Hoffman.

Bobby Seale's angry outbursts gradually intensified for not being able to have his own lawyer. His California lawyer was too sick to defend him at the time. On October 29, Judge Hoffman ordered Seale bound and gagged. On November 5, Judge Hoffman declared a mistrial for Bobby Seale. Dismissed from the trial, he was sentenced to four years in prison for contempt of court (which was overturned in 1972) and then he was sent to face another trial on the East Coast, this time for murder. Without Bobby Seale, the Chicago trial was renamed *The Conspiracy Seven*.

I was personally much relieved and felt that I could breathe easily now, since there would no longer be any chance that I would be subpoenaed to testify. Besides him disrupting the trial, I believe Seale had to be released from the trial, because Judge Hoffman realized there was no evidence of him meeting ahead of time, much less plotting revolt, with the planners of the demonstrations. How could he be charged with accepting an invitation to speak at three peaceful rallies—one on August 27, 1968 in Lincoln Park and the others on August 28 and 30 in Grant Park? Tapes of his speeches provided evidence that he was not inciting violence during anti-war protests, only righteous resistance and surly self-defense.

151

I learned later from reading his autobiography that he was held in Cook County Jail the entire time he was on trial, where he was treated like a dangerous criminal. (Seale, Bobby. *A Lonely Rage: The Autobiography of Bobby Seale.* New York: Times Books, 1978) I don't know where the other defendants stayed at night during the long months of the trail. Probably not in jail. Again I wondered, what is the real conspiracy here? Is it harassment of the Black Panthers?

Even though I thought I had to suspend my counseling sessions while I was ill, because they were in the Chicago Loop, I thought about them a lot. At first I didn't like to submit myself to the questions and insights of the counselor and it seemed like hard work. However, I came to feel that counseling was probably the best money I ever spent so far in my life. I read the second Eric Berne book that Mister Cofer had wanted me to read: *What Do You Say After You Say Hello?* My counselor had been helping me to clarify who I was, how my relationships with my parents still influenced my present day relationships, and what I wanted out of my life. He was the first adult person I ever remembered who listened to me talk at length without interrupting. He even identified my chosen mission in life was to be a peacemaker, the type that is a bridge between races and nationalities. *Beverly, the bridge! Beverly, the peacemaker!* I liked the vision, even though it was unclear in my mind.

I decided to ask to see my counselor every two weeks. My rationale was that my primary care physician had me come to see him twice a month at the hospital even though I was on bed rest, so I figured if I only went somewhere once a week, that the counseling trip was as emotionally healing as the physician trip was physically healing for me, After a couple of sessions, I wrote in my journal:

Mister Cofer said I have been depressed since the fall of '67 for two years now. When Randall (a fellow graduate student I had dated seriously) broke up with me, I turned my anger toward him inward, and my "punishing parent" told myself that I deserved losses like this one. Mr. Cofer says nobody deserves that, no human being deserves that. Then John came along; I was pulled out of depression, because John compensated for it on a deep level by punishing me emotionally in various ways. He scolded me, made me feel guilty, cost me money, kept me broke, etcetera. After each big "knock-out," what would I do? Go back for more! Actually, I used John to punish myself and treat myself like the heel I am convinced I am. Mr. Cofer said I am dealing with my extreme need for love differently now. Before Randall, I would cut guys off before they got too close. But with Randall, I allowed myself to open up and even talk about and imagine marriage, and then he broke up with me. Mister Cofer said that break-up removed all my props, and I became depressed. Now that depression remains below the surface—that's why I cry easily. But he says, I don't have to live with it. I can learn to give and receive the love I need. Start by concentrating on who loves me right now. Accept their love. Feel loved.

Yes, one of the cultural themes of the time was Make Love, Not War. But it was a really perplexing conundrum to try to identify where there was love in my generation and who might love me. Vietnam was affecting our whole generation. All young men between the ages of 18 and 26 were mandated to register for military service. Unless they got a deferment to go to college or got turned down because of a disability, they had to go away into the armed services. The young single men who interested me were activists, either in the war protest movement or the civil rights movement. They were not the loving types.

Even though I was lying flat on my back, my mind wandered to whether I could call myself an activist or not. Looking back, I assessed my own lifetime experiences in activism which consisted of participation in seven varied demonstrations. No two demonstrations were exactly alike, and all seven were effective in different ways, depending on the purpose.

1. In 1961 there was going to be a first ever demonstration for open housing at the state capitol building in Des Moines, Iowa. I told my boyfriend, Bob, about it and he responded enthusiastically, telling me what a wonderful opportunity we had to do something about racial discrimination, the greatest injustice of our time. Even though he went to a different college, he said he would drive to Ames and take me if I wanted to go. Dozens of college students drove to the Iowa state capitol building, got our placards with messages exposing unjust landlord practices, and were instructed to merely walk on the sidewalk around the periphery of the State Capitol for a couple hours.

   While Bob and I walked, I told him about the group on campus called the Student Committee on Racial Equality, SCORE for short. Prior to the demonstration, I had participated in a survey they conducted of all the homeowners listed with the college offering rooms to rent to students who wished to live off campus. First a foreign or non-Caucasian student with an accent would call to find out if a room was available for rent; then I was assigned to call and ask the same question. Those homeowners who were not amenable to "open housing" were identified. The college sent follow-up letters of warning after the demonstration.

   Photographers from the Des Moines Register newspaper took pictures that day, including one of Bob and me marching. Our picture appeared on the third page of the Sunday paper. My parents' only response was they hoped my extracurricular activities weren't interfering with my studies, but my brother and sister told me privately that the folks were shocked to see their daughter demonstrating and were somewhat embarrassed. This didn't really bother me, because I thought they also secretly approved. My parents had often invited an international college student to be our guest during Thanksgiving vacation, since they couldn't go home for those few days there were no classes. Our parents' hospitality introduced our guests to American customs and taught us children to show love to all people like the Sunday school chorus, "Red and yellow, black and white, all are precious in his sight. Jesus loves the little children of the world." I was doing what I had been taught.

The demonstration was successful. The college prepared a new list of "open housing opportunities" for off campus students. And I became an activist, thanks to SCORE and friends like Bob! Did Bob love me? He probably did, but I couldn't accept love at the time.

2-4. I joined in the Northwestern University student antiwar demonstration and the first two antiwar demonstrations in Lincoln Park, Bobby Seale was the featured speaker, invited to rally the troops and to present the rationale behind one of the biggest antiwar protests in the nation. What a speech! This was real protesting in my estimation, and I was Bobby Seale's driver! I walked to one rally with Carlos, and we felt a real camaraderie with each other. Was that love? Maybe it could have been, if we were closer in age.

5. I participated in a grape boycott in support of the United Farm Workers, a union trying to organize in California under the leadership of Cesar Chavez. Many church pastors including my pastor, Reverend Jim Neuman, recruited parishioners to demonstrate. One Saturday we went to a

Jewel grocery store, were given "Boycott Grapes" placards, and walked back and forth on the sidewalk in front of the store, being careful not to block the front door.

A poignant memory that day was a middle-aged man coming up to me and asking in apparent sincerity what we were protesting. I told him we were asking people not to buy California grapes in support of the farm workers. Then he asked me what was wrong with the conditions on the farms in California. I grew up on a farm in Iowa, but I didn't know about farms in California. I referred him to the leader of our demonstration, but he said, "No, that's okay. I just wondered. I thought you would know." I felt terrible that I couldn't answer his basic question about why we were doing what we were doing. I learned from that encounter that I wasn't going to protest anything else, no matter who asked me, unless I knew why I was doing it. And I applied a lifelong personal policy I learned from my mother on how to handle failure. Instead of wallowing in self-recrimination or blaming some-one else, I made it a point to learn what I could do to avoid the same failure again next time.

I went to Reverend Neuman and asked him to explain what the farm workers needed and how our boycotting grapes would help them. He told me to read the book *Grapes of Wrath* by John Steinbeck. I did, and it clearly portrayed how migrant families desperately needed to work to sur-vive. They converged on one farm after another to harvest fruit and cotton, were provided poor living quarters, all ages forced to work long hours, and no provision made for schooling or health care. They were not allowed to protest and forcefully stopped from joining any organization that would represent them with the land owners. Comparing my farm family life, where neighbors helped each other, to that of the migrant families, I was ashamed that those big business farmers would treat their workers that way.

They maximized their profits at the expense of the children and adults who worked for them with no regard for their suffering.

My own farm family did not own our farm, but we did have our freedom and we could count on having the basics of life. Planting and harvesting seasons were the two busiest times of the year. As soon as we children were about twelve years old, we were expected to help after school and in the summers doing chores, field work, and storing harvested crops for the winter. I extrapolated that migrant workers and their families lived their entire working lives in that heightened pressure of planting and harvesting, hard work, long days, and no relief from the hot sun, always moving on to a new site when one was completed. Migrant farm workers probably had one of the hardest jobs in the world.

6. Reverend Jim Neuman also got groups of us church members to attend Chicago city council hearings on neighborhood issues in Humboldt Park. He was active in the Saul Alinsky plan for grassroots community organizing, telling us city services would improve if the neighborhood residents showed concern for community matters. I got to know Reverend Neuman and his wife, Ruth, quite well; they invited me to supper with their family about once a week after I finished giving after-school piano lessons to their daughters Karin and Judy. I admired how the Neumans cared so deeply for the church and community, and put their whole selves into any project they considered important. They were my home away from home and a forever influence on my life. I loved them like my own family and I am sure they loved me, too.

7. The January1969 teacher strike was the first time I participated in a protest regarding my own job salary and working conditions. I was a brand-new teacher on my first full-time

job in Chicago, so I had no frame of reference. I relied on stories told by the "old-timers" to know why a strike had been deemed necessary. They considered this first ever teachers' strike in Chicago Public Schools to be a radical but necessary step since teachers were professionals who were not treated as professionals. The strike lasted about a week, while negotiations were held on working conditions, state funding issues, and establishment of a grievance procedure to hopefully prevent future strikes. Afterwards, my paycheck did take a jump up, which allowed me to save money to move to my own one-bedroom apartment near the church in Humboldt Park someday, to take a summer train trip out west to visit Helen, my former co-worker, and to dream of visiting other countries on other continents. It became evident to me that teachers are the main ingredient in education and our well-being was best protected by teacher unions even though unions were far from perfect.

Did anyone love me on the teaching staff? No, love and work were two different things. However, the visit out west to see Helen was because we were former co-workers who still loved each other as life-long friends. I remembered how concerned she was for my health and probably still was. I wrote her a letter to let her know how things were going.

I learned that my generation was referred to as the Silent Generation. We were those born between 1925 and 1945, sandwiched between the Greatest Generation, born in 1900 to 1924, and the Baby Boomers born from 1946 to1964. The latter were those born when the soldiers came home after World War II. Unlike the Greatest Generation, the Silent Generation did not win any important war, but like the Baby Boomers, we were children of war and children of the Depression. We grew up living impotently with the conflicts, fears, and sacrifices that wars caused. We were affected by rationing and we were brought up to submerge our own wants and needs to the common good. We became experts at long-term gratification and never even expected short-term gratification. No one cared if we had self-esteem (parents taught us to mind our manners); we were not addicted to self-expression (children are to be seen and not heard); we did accept self-sacrifice (military service was expected.) People of our generation were not very introspective, but were good followers, only thrust into leadership positions when there was a need, rather than being greedy for recognition. I wondered how a Silent Generation person could also be an activist. Maybe it was an all or nothing thing.

8. How could I forget one of the main events of my life? I gave four years of my life to activism. When President John Kennedy put out the call to young people to join the newly created Peace Corps, he ignited a flame from those burning embers. Most of my female friends and I joined either the Peace Corps or the Methodist Short-term Mission Program (two very similar programs) right after college graduation. We young women in particular wanted to be of service to our country or to be part of something bigger than ourselves. We wanted to work toward peace with justice in our world. The prophet Micah said, "What does the Lord require of you, but to do justice, love kindness, and walk humbly with your Lord?" We were the Silent Generation, but we were the Do It generation. Someone invented the saying: We walk the walk, not just talk the talk

I went back and re-read my journal entries for those four years. When I was in Mexico, actually starting with language training in Costa Rica, love became the quest of my life. I wrote about the observation that missionary people and church people were so joyful and loving. I did believe I could feel in retrospect the love of the Velasco family, who were my home away from home while I was in Chihuahua, Mexico. The Neuman family was becoming my favorite home away from home here in Chicago. I wondered how Mister Cofer knew how hard I had been trying to figure out what love was for a long time.

I was relieved when the doctor approved that I could drive my car to meet EJ and YJ at the airport upon their big return from Japan. They stayed with us in our Sheffield and Waveland apartment for a couple days as they recovered from jet lag. Erwin looked just like he did the last time I saw him but much more tanned from working outside in the hot tropical sun. Yoshiko was very tall, almost as tall as Erwin. She was as pretty as a Japanese doll. Her English was excellent and easy to understand. Rachel, Erwin, Yoshiko, and I went shopping to find her something fashionable in American style. We discovered her clothing size was only a Misses' size three and very few stores carried size three. I bought them a wedding present they said they needed—a rice steamer.

My mother's Christmas letter that year to friends and relatives most clearly described the exuberance we all felt at the family get-together that year.

> *Our family circle was complete around a holiday table this past Thanksgiving, for the first time since 1965. We were joined by other relatives for a celebration, which nearly burst out the walls. It was a "mountaintop experience."*

> *This was a joyous year for the Johnsons. Our hearts are filled with gratitude for so many blessings: the safe return of our beloved son, Erwin, and his lovely bride, Yoshiko; Beverly on the road to recovery; a bountiful crop, though late, harvested safely; Beverly drove her car home bringing Erwin and Yoshiko, after two days spent in Chicago celebrating their arrival in the US at O'Hare International*

Airport on Sunday, November 23rd. How I would have loved to join Beverly and Rachel's "Welcome Home" to them with flowers and joyous hugs, but we were still picking corn, as well as expecting carpenters who were putting in the footings and foundation in for an addition to our home.

We were able to fulfill Erwin's dream of driving in the lane of our home and being greeted by the smell of fresh, homemade bread, along with the tears of joy. The sorrow of parting is almost forgotten in the ecstasy of reunion. His delightful bride is very easy to love, and include in our family circle. We are gradually learning of their life in Laos, their stay in Japan including a Japanese wedding ceremony, in addition to their official marriage at the American Embassy in Vientiane, Laos, while they are adjusting to life here in the States.

Beverly did finish her M.A. requirements this year, but succumbed to a recurrence of the rheumatic fever she first endured at six years of age. She will soon resume her teaching responsibilities at Waller High, in inner-city Chicago, as she has been gradually regaining her strength and freedom from rheumatic pain.

Rachel is teaching Spanish and English in a large high school in Cicero, Illinois. She likes the school since the teachers' strike at the beginning of the school year has been settled. Her health is much improved since she underwent a lengthy series of allergy tests and knows what to avoid. She is still in therapy, but is a good mother to Markie, a husky, healthy, happy, intelligent little two year old "go-getter." What joy and fun Grandma and Grandpa derive from this precious addition to our family circle.

Last, but certainly not least, Sydnee is adding another fine young man to our family circle. She is in her second year at the University of Iowa at Iowa City, and plans to be married on February 14th to a young man farming with his father near Davenport, Iowa. Many happy plans are afoot. She and John are already furnishing a nice, large house on one of the farms his family owns.

Herb and I are keeping busy with church, Farm Service, and Farm Bureau activities. I have one more responsibility before Christmas, to attend the American Farm Bureau Convention at the Washington Hilton, Washington D.C. One of the exciting privileges will be a tea at the White House with Pat Nixon as hostess. My other deeply satisfying responsibilities are Junior High church school teacher, choir director, part-time church organist, and member of the church official board, and Herb is chairman of the Audit Committee and Recording Secretary of the official board.

Our Christmas heritage is rich beyond words in the things that really count in this life. Let's dedicate ourselves to take the sweetness of Christmas with us throughout the year and flavor all the other days.

Affectionately, Herb and Thelma Johnson.

In marked contrast to the joy of our family Thanksgiving, there was yet another shocking murder on December 4 in Chicago. The charismatic chairman of the Illinois Black Panther Party, Fred Hampton, and another leader, Mark Clark, were shot and killed as they slept in their beds by a special Chicago police unit in an early morning raid on their Chicago apartment. Even though there were many differences in the factors and conditions surrounding this killing, there were also some eerie similarities with the Bruce and Eugenia Johnson killings. Both were targeted on controversial leaders; both were carried out under cover of darkness. A big difference was that the Chicago Police were openly identified in newspaper accounts as the ones that led the raid, because it was officially believed that the apartment held a cache of guns and deadly weapons, and the Chicago Police Department and the F.B.I. would carry out the investigation of this most recent killing. Followers of Fred Hampton immediately called Foul! The very next day they called a press conference where the raid took place, standing on the front porch of the house and pointing out that all the shots came from the outside in. They blamed the government and the policemen. They proclaimed, "You can kill the revolutionary, but you cannot kill the revolution."

Posters started appearing with quotes attributed to Fred Hampton and pictures of him. Some of the most popular ones went like this:

> You have to understand that people have to pay the price for peace. You dare to struggle, you dare to win. If you dare not struggle, then goddammit it, you don't deserve to win.

> You don't fight fire with fire. You fight fire with water. We're gonna fight racism with solidarity.

> Let me just say: Peace to you, if you're willing to fight for it.

> *–Fred Hampton*

This story was far from over. The news would come out later of some activists in Pennsylvania who did something about the extreme number of casualties of peacemaking and the unprovoked killings in this country in the 1960s. With more courage and tenacity than I could have ever imagined, they looked in an unsuspecting place for the cause. Some attributed their energizing and radicalization to the official killing raid of Fred Hampton and Mark Clark. Their deaths may have been the "straw that broke the camel's back."

CHAPTER 10
Bouncing Back

WINTER, 1970

Once I was back at work after Christmas vacation, it was like starting a new school year. I was more than ready to focus my renewed health and energy into my classes and the students and make teaching my number one priority. For my New Year's resolution, I brought the students' papers home to grade and lesson plans to create rather than stay after school as I had done my first year. The difference was that I first ate supper with my roommates and then settled down to work on paperwork every night in front of the television set, as I continued my new habit of watching the nightly news and my favorite programs. And no more Saturday or Sunday jobs.

Just as I had started living into my New Year's resolution, my department chair offered me the chance to develop a home economics after-school program, if I wanted it. It was only supposed to be like one more class, a tenth period. The advantage for me was that I needed the money (20 percent added to my salary check) to pay back my graduate school loans. I thought the advantage of getting paid to spend creative time with students far outweighed the disadvantage of putting in an extra forty-five minutes at school. So I said, "Yes" while making myself a promise to make no more exceptions to my rule to take care of myself.

The home economics after-school program was called Home Project and Visitation Program and included sponsoring a club called Future Homemakers of America (FHA). Any student enrolled in a home economics class could choose to join the after-school program. About twenty girls signed up. They came in for an extra period after ninth period class Tuesday through Thursday to work on a project of their choice that would improve their home. Some chose to make a piece of clothing for a younger brother or sister. Some chose to make curtains, dresser scarves, or pillows for their parents' apartment or house. I was supposed to do home visits, when the opportunity came up.

Immediately I discovered how I had to "switch gears" in my attitude toward working with the students. In the after-school program, I did not have to be a disciplinarian. The girls were there because they wanted to be there and they were trying to do something to better their lives. My role was to listen to them, discern whether their proposed project was appropriate and possible, and guide them in the steps needed to accomplish it. I felt as though I were taking off my policeman hat and letting my guard down. I didn't have to always be ready to react to someone breaking rules, because no one did. I hadn't realized before how much I felt like a policeman-teacher during the school day. I wished I could soften up a bit in classroom teaching, but I knew they would take advantage of me if I did. The after-school program turned out to be one of the most satisfying things I did as a teacher. The home visits were particularly memorable.

Betty was in her second year of Textiles and Clothing. She wanted to make colorful curtains for the kitchen in her family's apartment. I instructed her how to take the measurements of the windows, decide how much fabric to buy, and then I answered her questions as she machine-sewed the curtains as fast as she could.

When she finished, she took them home and the next day, she was bubbling over as she came to see me before school started.

"The curtains are beautiful in our windows, Miss Johnson. My mother loves them. You should see them. Can you make us a home visit? Can you? Can you?"

"Sure, I'd love to. You're the first to invite me. Where do you live?"

"On the 8th floor in Cabrini Greens. My address is 1230 North Burling. Can you come next week?"

Betty met me after school and she rode with me in my car. I parked on the street in front of one of many Cabrini-Green high rise apartment buildings in the area. A large group of black children and young people were standing in front of the main entrance of 1230 N. Burling. Betty greeted them and they greeted her and all said hello to me, some giggling. As Betty and I walked into the building, the mass of young people followed us closely to the elevator. We waited while the elevator rumbled down to the first floor. A couple of men walked off, scowling at the children. Then the whole group of us crowded noisily into the elevator and began our ascent. When the elevator stopped on a floor, everyone would laugh and say this elevator was full. Arriving on the 8th floor, we all got off en masse. Betty and I went into the apartment. The rest of the children and teens waited outside the apartment in the hallway.

Betty's mother was a gracious hostess and said she was so proud of her daughter. I raved about how well made the curtains were and how they perked up the kitchen beautifully. Her mother said she thought their apartment looked much better. She took me on a tour of the rest of the apartment which consisted of three bedrooms, a dining room, and a bathroom. Betty had three younger brothers and sisters who watched us and listened quietly.

After the fifteen-minute home visit, we left the apartment and there was the same mob of children and teens as before. We again walked *en masse* to the elevator; all piled in, and made our descent back to first floor. They walked me to my car and waved good-bye.

The next day I told my fellow home economics teachers about the experience. They looked horrified.

"You went up into THE Cabrini Greens? It's a wonder you got out alive. They're dangerous, you know."

"No, I didn't. That must be the reason for all those kids crowding into the elevator until it was full. No one else could get in."

"They were protecting you, young lady. They must like you. At least they don't want you to become a casualty of gang war." We all laughed, but my laugh sounded hollow in my ears. That comment made me realize how vulnerable I had been. I was grateful for the advance planning by Betty and her mother, and decided to require something like that of all future home visits.

I started asking around and found out that Cabrini-Greens was a public housing complex, originally with a long waiting list, which included blacks, whites, and Hispanics. The "projects" run by the Chicago Housing Authority had the noble purpose of replacing ramshackle poverty housing and giving families a decent affordable place to live. Although there were 15,000 residents including a lot of children and teens, I noticed there were no parks, playgrounds, or community centers. There were just fifteen high rise apartment buildings located between Lincoln Park and the Gold Coast. When gang graffiti began to appear everywhere, the waiting lists evaporated. After Martin Luther King was assassinated, snipers positioned themselves on the upper floors of the high rise buildings and shot at each other and at people on the sidewalks. There had been a number of casualties and considerable property damage. This was the environment in which many of the African

American students in Waller High School lived and had to survive in order to attend school.

✴

During my bout with rheumatic fever, because I lost touch with all my friends except my church friends, I needed to make new friends. I also knew I had to get back to being physically active, so I decided to check out the American Youth Hostels (AYH) center in my north side neighborhood near Wrigley Field. Compared to laid-back pot parties, AYH activities were organized, done in daylight hours, outdoors, activity-based, and had no dress code! I took up hiking—beginning with half-day hikes in forest preserves.

On a brisk winter hike in a forest preserve I found myself walking beside a tall slender guy about my age. He walked with a bounce and talked easily, even though we were walking fairly fast. We found we both lived near Wrigley Field. All of the sudden, he stepped ahead of me, turned 180 degrees, and faced me. He had a sly grin.

"I have a claim to fame in Wrigleyville."

"Oh, yeah? What's that?"

"I'm the Republican precinct captain."

"Please tell me what that is, so I can be properly impressed. I'm not even registered to vote in Chicago."

"The precinct captain is responsible for getting out the Republican vote."

"Far out. I didn't know there were any Republicans in Chicago. I was planning to register as a Democrat, since it looks like the real election is in the primaries."

My new friend laughed. "Are you a Democrat?"

"No, I plan to vote for the candidate, not the party. I guess that makes me an independent."

"There might be more Republicans than you think. You really don't know any?"

"Actually I do. My family in Iowa is all Republican. The first time I ever voted, my mother had a Republican primary ballot sent to me."

His eyes brightened. "How would you like to help me canvas the vote?"

"How can I? I'm not registered."

"Don't worry about that. You can do that later. I'll give you a list of all the registered Republican voters in one city block. You go out canvassing around suppertime and knock on doors. If someone answers the door, you ask if you can count on their vote. If anyone there is not on your list, you ask, no, you encourage them to register to vote. You'll have cards that tell them when and where they can go sign up to vote in the next election. You can register yourself that way."

"That sounds simple enough. Sure, I'll give it a try."

Smiling like a Cheshire cat, he reached out his hand to shake mine. "All right, there is actually a bit more to it. I'd like to take you out for dinner some evening after Election Day, you know, to thank you and talk about the election."

"That's cool. By the way, my name is Beverly. What's your name?"

"Larry—at your service." He bowed deeply from his hips. I looked at him a little more critically. He wasn't bad looking. His six-foot frame was slender and athletic, his sandy hair wind-blown. He looked like a contemporary Abe Lincoln in hiking shorts and shirt. I liked his enthusiasm, his good humor, and his seeming intelligence.

Starting the very next week, Larry assigned me to the block in which I lived. Most people on the list lived in apartment buildings like me. I found twice as many unregistered voters as registered voters. Many of them spoke no English and I didn't speak Polish. Some acted as though they were suspicious of me, even though I couldn't have appeared official in any way. I wore blue jeans and a blouse, and approached the residents with my Iowa friendliness. Sometimes I got the door slammed in my face. I began to wonder if maybe they were covering up that they weren't citizens. I also wondered if this was worth doing just to get a date with Larry.

On Primary Election Day, he asked me to work as a poll watcher for the Republicans in the precinct voting place. Larry pointed out the Democratic precinct captain. He was a guy in his fifties, dressed in work clothes, who later came over and asked what I was doing.

"I'm a poll watcher."

"I know." He shook his head. "What are you doing, being a **Republican**?"

"I'm working for Larry, you know, the Republican precinct captain."

"Yeah, yeah. But you're the same age as my kids. You're not rich. I still say, what're you doing, being a **Republican**?"

"My family in Iowa is all Republican."

"But what about you? Republicans aren't going to do anything for **you**. They don't even see poor people like **you**."

Then he chuckled to himself, "I'm gonna become a Republican someday, too, when my ship comes in." He walked away still chuckling and shaking his head.

✷

Larry and I did go out for dinner after the primaries. We talked about how we were different from people we knew who were involved in the hippie movement.

"I guess I'm different mostly, because I tried marihuana, but I just can't get into drugs. How about you, Larry?"

"Same here. I don't think there is a real hippie movement here in the Midwest. Maybe I'm wrong, but I think you'd have to move to Oakland, California, or Greenwich Village in New York City to live in a commune where free sex and drugs is a life style," Larry answered.

"I want to be more than a 'rebel without a cause.' How did President Kennedy put it? 'Ask not what your country can do for you; ask what you can do for your country.' My mission is working with inner-city kids."

"There really are lots of ways to serve. You can teach inner-city kids; you can go into politics, demonstrate against the war, sign up for Peace Corps … " Larry made the peace symbol to me.

I made the peace symbol back to him. "Yeah, and peace is more than the absence of war. I believe peacemaking means learning to get along with people of other races and nationalities, in other countries and right here at home."

By then, we were finished eating and Larry suggested he could come over to my place for a little while. I liked him, so I said yes, innocently, assuming my roommates Rachel and Janice would be there. When we got there, no one was home. I asked him if he wanted a Coke.

His response unexpectedly surprised me. "Forget about that. The hippies are right about something: our sexual taboos are too strict, way too strict. I bought you a good dinner to thank you for working with me. It's your turn to thank me back."

With that statement, his hands were all over me. He pushed me down on the couch. I was shocked. The look on his face was determined, not romantic or caring or fun-loving any more. I was going to get raped, if I didn't do something fast.

"No, not now!" I demanded. I had always thought I was strong since I was a farm girl, but I discovered that even a skinny city guy had a lot more strength than I did. He was holding me down firmly. I was going to have to give in, or think of something to distract him.

I started to laugh my crazy witch laugh I had perfected long ago with my younger brother and sister when we were children. He stopped and stared at me, his eyes and mouth wide open.

"Are you all right?"

I laughed eerily again, rolling my eyes at him.

"Uh, I better get going. Maybe we can get together again some other time."

Larry never again called me for a date or for political work. During the actual election that next fall, I joined the Independent Precinct Organization (IPO) that was handing out flyers to elect Bill Singer, an independent candidate for Alderman in the 35th Ward.

I confided in Janice about my near rape experience and how I felt betrayed. I had thought Larry needed help with getting voters to the polls and something might come out of it, but all along, he was just expecting some political help and cheap sex. Janice and I agreed that we didn't know how to pick men. We felt stuck in a rut, because we didn't want to date any of the men we knew from church or work. Actually, that wasn't totally true. I enjoyed going to listen to one teacher, a jazz piano player on the side, in the club where he was playing. He told me he liked me, but he was contracted with a Jewish matchmaker to get his bride. He was waiting for a promised match from Michigan.

Janice showed me an ad she cut out of the newspaper for a company called Computer Dating. This was a new use of computers to match men and women with similar interests and goals. We ordered the forms and filled out the five-page questionnaire about demographics, favorite activities, value systems, religious preferences, and dating goals. I had to decide if my ultimate goal was marriage, love, or just meeting new people. I checked the latter, although down deep, I wished it could be love. Janice checked meeting new people, too. We also had to decide on the age span and race of our potential matches. We both put down white and/or black men and she chose an older age span than I did. We each sent in our forms with a bank check for thirty dollars, a lot of money in those days. The computer work was done at their company and we were guaranteed three matches. We assumed we were in for some adventures.

About ten days later, we both got letters in the mail from Computer Dating with six names each, three white guys and three black guys. Instructions were that we were to wait for the guys to call us. The calls began almost immediately, and Betty had the first date, a black guy who arrived at the apartment to pick her up on a big Harley motorcycle. My first date was a white guy who lived about three blocks away and walked over. Back then there was no place to eat around Wrigley Field, so we walked several blocks to a café on Broadway Avenue. I tried to think of things to talk about, but it was difficult. I knew that I was somewhat shy, but he had trouble talking about anything at all.

My first black date was a jazz musician. We went to listen to a jazz group playing at a downtown hotel venue and thoroughly enjoyed the evening. We went together to some other jazz events around the city and it seemed that a black and white couple was considered "cool" in jazz circles. One time I needed someone to cover for me at my Sunday church organist job and my jazz friend agreed to do so. Reverend Neuman then asked him if he could continue to come and help him start a Sunday afternoon service to appeal to African American families in Humboldt Park. Eventually I asked him to take over my organist job at the Sunday morning worship services, which he did. It gave him a steady Sunday gig and it gave me a day off work every week to better protect my health.

My jazz musician friend and I never did anything romantic, not even a kiss, but two of my other date matches made up for it. A European white guy wined me and dined me at Lawry's, a high-end steak restaurant on the Gold Coast. Then he was straightforward with me, telling me that afterward we were to go to his apartment for drinks and sex. When I declined, he took me home, saying I should call him if I ever changed my mind. Otherwise, it was good-bye. I didn't call him, even though I wondered what it would be like to lose my virginity in such a business arrangement.

Another black guy took me straight to his apartment on the south side, explaining that he rented the whole floor himself and then sub-let rooms to single working women. He introduced me to them and showed me a room he had for rent. Talk about business arrangements with probable sex expectations. I sensed there was some jealousy and hurt feelings among the women. He was handsome, but I was very uneasy while we watched some television in his master bedroom, I could hear the women walking back and forth in the hallway. After a while, I told him I had to leave and go home.

The third white guy raised my suspicions on the phone, because he wouldn't reveal anything personal about himself, such as where he lived and worked, and he said he didn't have a home phone. He called me several times from a pay phone in the corner tavern. I didn't trust that he was telling the truth, so I never met him. The third black guy was head cook in a restaurant on the third floor of the Prudential Building, one of the tallest skyscrapers in

Chicago at the time. He drove me all around Chicago, showing me Chicago sites I had never explored, such as Lower Wacker Drive, Chicago River north and south branches, Chicago River locks, Lake Michigan beaches on the far South Side, Midway Airport, the area of Chicago called Beverly, and the University of Chicago campus. He was fun to be with and had a good sense of humor, but we never went anywhere around other people. I assumed he felt uncomfortable in public with a white woman, whether we were around blacks or whites. We never talked about that.

It seemed as though everyone my age was having sex. However, my value system was to wait to have sex until I married. I didn't feel I could just start having sex without at least being engaged to be married. I hadn't met anyone I wanted to marry for so long that I thought I might never marry. However, I didn't know why God would give me hormones and desires for sex, if it was going to be a lifetime taboo. I wrote extensively in my journal about this confusion, but never talked to anyone except my counselor about it. Even though I had just met six guys with whom Computer Dating deemed I was well matched, the only two I liked well enough to date more than once were the jazz musician and the cook, and I couldn't see myself getting serious about either one. I just wanted to meet a fun-loving intelligent guy of any race with whom I could have a good healthy relationship. I would learn to love him and counseling would help me.

The Conspiracy Eight trial minus one, Bobby Seale, now re-named the Conspiracy Seven by the newspapers and on television, meant I didn't have to worry about being called in to testify anymore, but I continued to follow it and also the continuing news of Bobby Seale. *Jet Magazine* reported he was transported to an eastern state to face charges of murder. Seale was eventually acquitted due to trumped up charges and circumstantial evidence. It seemed similar to the case of Cassius Clay (Mohammed Ali) who was sent to prison for refusing the draft and was stripped of his heavyweight boxing title. It seemed to me that blacks got more than their share of severe charges and jail punishment not befitting the crime.

In the whole process of the Chicago Eight/Seven grand jury hearing and trial, I felt a certain empathy toward Bobby Seale as opposed to Abby Hoffman and Jerry Rubin. The latter two had to create a scene in order to get into trouble with police and get media attention. Bobby had only to show up and act like who he was—an angry, self-confident, vocal, intelligent black man and for this, he stayed in trouble. The Black Panther's contention that young black men were treated much worse in law enforcement situations than were other races did not stretch my credulity too far.

As a young woman driving and walking around Chicago during those years, I felt some of the unfairness of discrimination. Later they would call it profiling, but being a tall, slender, young white woman, and apparently not too hard to look at, I must have stood out going places by myself in the city. Every time I walked past a construction site, I tried my best to ignore the whistles and cat calls.

I thought I was treated so unfairly one time that I wrote a complaint letter to the editor of the Chicago Daily News. I told how I was walking down my neighborhood street, when a squad car pulled up beside me. I might have caught his eye, because I was wearing one of my first conspicuous purchases with my salary check—a black leather jacket. The police officer spoke out his side window, asking me where I was going. I said I was walking home from the bus stop. I kept on walking and he continued driving beside me, talking about smart aleck young people causing all the troubles in Chicago and making it difficult for law enforcement. It was scary. He followed me to the end of the block before he drove off. My letter to the newspaper was printed.

The policeman assigned to Waller High School looked me up with that newspaper in hand and asked if I wrote that letter. I admitted it somewhat sheepishly. He laughed and told me I had a lot of courage. After that, it made me feel a little safer during the school day that I could call on him directly if I needed help with any school situation that could erupt at any time. One time I was driving down the expressway, when I saw police car lights flashing behind me. I thought, *oh, no, what did I do wrong now? I had better change my whole style of driving, so I can quit getting so many tickets.* A driver could only get two tickets in one calendar year, because on the third, you had to appear in court and might lose your driver's license. That time it was just my school policeman friend, who laughed and asked me if I had ever been stopped for driving perfectly.

The worst incident was earlier one night when John was riding with me in my car; I got stopped by the police for making a left turn without putting on my turn signal. He said he would have to take me to the police station under suspicion of DUI (driving under the influence.) My sobriety test was to blow into a nozzle connected to a machine. The needle didn't budge. He had me do it again. Even though the results were zero, I couldn't believe it, when the policeman wrote down 0.01 on the scale. Then I had to stand with my arm out, close my eyes, and touch my nose with my index finger. I had to walk about ten feet on a straight line. Finally, I had to say the words: Methodist Episcopal. I was beginning to think it was funny until he told me I had failed, and I had to sign his report. I objected, but he said I had to sign it. So I wrote, "The above statements are false" and signed my name beneath my objection. He was livid. To avoid being sent to women's jail that night, I had to post cash bail bond. It was much more money than I had on me, so I used my one permitted call to call my pastor to see if he could come to the police station and lend me the bail money. He did bring the money to the police station. I knew I would be forever grateful for that kindness, which was far above and beyond what most people ask of their pastors. To make matters worse, the police assigned me to appear in felony court located on 22nd and California, rather than traffic court.

I took a day off work for the first court appearance. The defendants before me were accused of murder and robbery. When I was called to stand before him, the judge was very upset with me, because I was in the wrong court. Next I was sent to traffic court, where my case was continued two more times, because the arresting officer never showed up. The second time I questioned the judge about his absence, telling him that each time I had to miss a day of work. He was very abrupt with me saying, "Don't you want to hear what the arresting officer has to say?" I answered, "No." He said, "Case continued." The third time I decided I would have to hire one of the court lawyers plying their services out in the vestibule of the traffic court building. It cost me most of the bail money, which I had already paid. With the lawyer at my side, the case against me was dropped by the traffic court judge. I thought there was no lesson to be learned. The deck was stacked, and it was just my bad luck. But a black teacher told me I had learned the hard way the meaning of DWI and DWB, not "driving while intoxicated," but "driving while black."

with a crack?

✳

I was curious about the seven defendants accused of being the Conspiracy Seven, who were required to give up several months of their lives to stand trial, because they organized the immense amount of antiwar sentiment that existed among young people in America. I learned that the demonstrations were planned by two very different types of war protest leaders:

Rennie Davis first presented his vision for the Democratic Convention protest at a meeting he called at the University of Chicago in November 1967. His idea was to invite college student war protesters from all over the country to come to Chicago to demonstrate nonviolently against the nomination of President Lyndon Johnson and any other Democratic candidate who promoted winning the war in Vietnam. He convinced a group of like-minded young people to work with him to contact college protest groups. They named themselves MOBE or National Mobilization to End the War in Vietnam.

Two protest leaders from the East coast, Abbie Hoffman and Jerry Rubin, got a lot more media attention through counter-culture, freewheeling anti-establishment rabble rousing. They founded a group called Youth International Party, popularly known as YIPPIES to attract young people from all walks of life. They planned an event in Lincoln Park which would highlight the general discontent among our generation, including the opposition to the Vietnam War. On August 25, 1968, the Sunday night after I left for Iowa, they held their Festival of Life with music, flowers, pot, and poetry. Police had posted eleven o'clock curfew signs on park trees after a federal district judge denied the antiwar activists' request to camp out in the park. The judge denied their appeal for an injunction against the new park curfew. The event ended with police clearing the park with billy clubs and tear gas grenades. It was repeated the next night. The leaders were getting the media attention they wanted. And it started to become clear that most of the conflicts between police and protesters were due to the newly created curfew and police uncertainty about crowd control, once thousands of demonstrators were kicked out of the parks. (Kusch, Frank. *Battleground Chicago: The Police and the Democratic National Convention*. The University of Chicago Press: Chicago, 2008, pgs. 61-68.)

I figured the first training rally in which I participated that summer was probably led by a YIPPIE. He was preparing us in how to confront police if they tried to break up a group of us. Even though I wanted to demonstrate against the war, I felt I was being swept along into a type of protest I didn't want to do, because I saw my choice as either-or: go along with the confrontational approach or not partici-pate at all. For me, the confrontational approach was too much. For others, it was not enough. That was where I first heard angry grum-bling that nothing would work until "we bring the war home."

I didn't know what I would have chosen to do on Friday, the first day of public demonstrations, if another opportunity hadn't come along, in which I could help out in a more constructive way. That was when I gave Bobby Seale and his bodyguards the ride to the Lincoln Park rally where he was the featured speaker.

The more I thought more about it, the more I realized how important that little task of mine was for the peace movement. Bobbie Seale was from the west coast and therefore symbolized unity between east and west, as well as between blacks and whites. His presence brought members of the Illinois Black Panther Party on board. Whites and blacks were in equal numbers in the crowd that night; they were loud, but totally peaceful that first night.

When the daytime and early evening rallies in Lincoln Park were going to move to downtown Chicago's Grant Park, I demurred. On one hand, I wanted to go on demonstrating, but didn't like that uncomfortable feeling about the tenor of the antiwar movement. I also thought I had done enough for one summer. I drove home to Iowa and missed out on the rest of the Democratic Convention; therefore, I missed out on confrontations with police. The leaders of the demonstrations were arrested several times, but I'm sure they never expected to spend five months in a Chicago courtroom prohibited from talking about a war that was still escalating.

The strange part was that each side had such different agendas that made the Conspiracy Seven trial as unwinnable as the Vietnam War. The war protest leaders did their best to put the establishment on trial with the general public. Judge Hoffman prohibited any antiwar propaganda in his courtroom. While more and more young men were being sent to Vietnam, he was not going to allow this trial to interfere with the American military efforts abroad or police efforts to keep stability in Chicago. So the judge was successful in keeping the trial focused on the obscure, but important amendment to the 1964 Civil Rights Act that prohibited people from crossing state lines to cause a riot. Did they or didn't they? Or was it actually the police that caused the riot in their overly ambitious crowd control tactics?

It all seemed to come down to a conflict between two generations of war cultures. The draft age group protesting the Vietnam War considered themselves victims, sacrificial lambs in a war with no ending, no resolution, and no benefits. The World War II veterans who now ran the government, the courts, and the military had served in a crucial war; most were extremely patriotic and simply did not seem to understand that Vietnam was not the same kind of war. The older citizens believed in the depths of their souls that, right or wrong, America always wins its wars. The younger citizens saw the risks and consequences of this war as too great; the older citizens saw any risk as a necessary component of war when serving and protecting one's country. But the Conspiracy Seven trial wasn't about the Vietnam War.

The Conspiracy Seven trial lasted for six months. Most people including myself lost interest in it. It finally ended and went to jury deliberations. On February 20, 1970 after one week of deliberations, the jury acquitted all of the policemen of charges of assault and battery. The jury acquitted all the demonstrators of conspiracy charges, but found five of the defendants guilty of crossing state lines to incite a riot. Judge Hoffman sentenced the five defendants to five years of imprisonment plus a $5,000 fine. He sentenced Bobby Seale and the defense attorneys, William Kunstler and Leonard Weinglass, to four years and thirteen days in jail for 159 incidents of criminal contempt of court. Mister Kunstler was the one I had met a year ago, who had advised me so accurately on how my brother could avoid military service after doing International Voluntary Service as a conscientious objector. I was glad to hear that they were going to appeal.

The appeal was finally settled on November 21, 1972 when the Seventh Circuit Court of Appeals overturned the sentences imposed on the two defense attorneys and Bobby Seale, because contempt convictions of more than six months required separate jury trials. It reversed the five defendants' convictions based on the judge's refusal to allow cultural bias questions in jury selection, also the judge's deprecatory attitude toward the defense, and evidence that the FBI, working with Judge Hoffman and prosecutors, had illegally bugged the offices of the Chicago Seven defense attorneys.

Telephone bugging was just what I had suspected happened to me. Then I wondered, if I was not a suspect according to the FBI agent who said I wasn't and if they did indeed bug our home telephone, wouldn't that be illegal, too?

I wondered if anyone won or anyone lost in that lengthy trial. Was it, as Carlos had said way back when we were walking away from the Lincoln Park rally, that everyone had to decide if they were for the revolution or for the establishment? Did everyone get sucked into this faux conflict? Did the city government and its police force believe the hippies and war protesters were there to start a revolution? If so, then they felt they won, because they stopped it by brute force and by not letting the conflicts on the streets stop the Democratic Convention. Did the war protesters win because they proved that the establishment was more warlike than anyone thought they were? If so, did anyone learn anything from this whole costly game played out in the courts? I didn't think so. It seemed like a big waste of time and money, trying to turn a big generational divide into all-out faux-war. It was not conflict resolution by win-lose; it was conflict resolution resulting in lose-lose. No one won.

I couldn't help but compare those two major events of my life that summer of 1968. The Democratic Convention war protests were lose-lose. Mayor Daley's Peace Corps summer program was win-win. I could imagine what Reverend Johnson saw when he looked over our little group of young adult summer school teachers that last day of summer school—twelve individuals who didn't know each other when the summer began, blacks and whites and Latinos who had never had much experience working with the other races. We were united by two things—the need for a paying summer job and a desire to help teenagers younger than ourselves. Reverend Johnson got us to work together for a common goal; he helped us reach it by guiding us to settle our differences along the way, and finding that we even came to care about each other.

When the impossible came to pass, he may have thought, "Here before my very eyes is a glimpse of the Kingdom of God on earth."

I wondered where Mayor Daley got the idea for the Mayor Daley's Peace Corps Program. When I went back into counseling, I got my answer one day, when I met another counselor in the office who told me he had been a member of Mayor Daley's Community Planning Advisory Committee. He explained to me their assigned task was to create ideas and recommend ways to "keep the peace" in Chicago before and during the Democratic Convention. The group, consisting of pastors, teachers, counselors, community leaders, and policemen, worked hard to come up with ways to prevent riots as happened in Los Angeles and to counteract any trouble in Chicago, such as what followed Martin Luther King's assassination. The weather prediction had been for a long hot summer.

He said their committee came up with remarkably innovative ideas, of which a few were accepted by Mayor Daley. One idea was to have the Chicago Fire Department release the locks on fire hydrants in certain neighborhood areas where gangs congregated outside corner taverns. As soon as the neighborhood children discovered this free fun, the potential troublemakers who hung out on those corners were replaced by laughing, screaming children and their watchful mothers. All it cost the city was water, which came abundantly from Lake Michigan anyway.

Another idea was the Mayor Daley Peace Corps Program itself. It was also very cost-effective and hugely successful. It was held in volunteer churches that wanted local missions in their communities. All participants except the pastors in charge were paid through federal work program funds. The students were paid the minimum wage which was $1.15 an hour at the time to learn to become productive Chicago citizens. We teachers were paid $1.60

an hour from the same federal work program fund. It was a reasonable summer job pay for me for the chance to learn to work with Chicago teenagers.

We worked together to make our little part of Chicago a better place for everyone. I tried to make the political process in Chicago come alive for the students and help them discover the need for their becoming involved eventually. We helped them discover pride in their own Puerto Rican history and culture. We inspired them to continue high school with the goal of graduating. None of us could have done these amazing things alone. Together we showed ourselves and the larger community the potential of working together to build bridges between cultures. And we were just average young people.

The whole summer program was a win-win-win situation. Mayor Daley won, because he kept the peace in neighborhoods that formed a ring around the Loop and saved the image of the city of Chicago he wanted to present to the world. Idle youth won, because they earned some money, stayed in school, and were empowered to become future community leaders. We young adults won, because we got to have teaching experience, earned some money, and had a unique interracial multi-cultural experience in a city and world that was still very segregated.

I didn't think much about it at the time, never even making a comment in my journal, but I now realize that the summer program changed my life and I think it changed the lives of my fellow teachers. We were ahead of our time in participating in a model that might well be replicated. What did we succeed in learning and doing?

- Treating each other as equals
- Being open and as honest as possible about our differences and prejudices

- Accepting differences without judging
- Working together to reach a goal
- Being empowered and encouraged in our work, but never criticized
- Having the program directors give us our assignments and letting us carry them out
- Having fun in the classroom and community

I became truly comfortable that summer in that multi-cultural situation, so much that I almost forgot what it was like to live in a mono-cultural community. I was changing to become more open-minded, embracing diversity, without realizing I was giving up my old ethnocentric ways forever.

One day I received a letter from the office of the doctor I had been seeing to cure my rheumatic fever. It was a bill for the money I still owed him, with a threat that I would be taken to court if I did not pay it immediately. It also announced that any future appointments were hereby cancelled. It was signed by his wife. I couldn't believe the abruptness and lack of explanation. So I called the hospital and learned he was deceased. They said they were not at liberty to tell me anything more. I couldn't think of any way to learn more, but I did remember one appointment when he asked me a couple of strange questions, "Are you depressed? Have you ever felt like ending your life?" I answered, "Depressed, yes. Commit suicide, no." I realized that serious depression could be a mental illness and that doctors are not immune; they are human, too. I knew I was becoming more sensitive to what other people were going through. I was glad I was in counselling.

CHAPTER 11
End-of-College Days

SPRING-SUMMER, 1970

The after-school club and students in the clothing classes had just finished one of our final rehearsals for the fashion show in the school auditorium. I made sure all the students left the school building and I walked out of the front door of Waller High School. My stomach suddenly screamed with pain. *What was happening to me? Where did that horrible pain come from?* As I unlocked the car door and climbed into my trusty Tough Buddy, I realized I hadn't eaten anything all day, because I was so busy trying to take care of all the details I needed to do and the students had so many individual questions and problems. A teacher had given me a packet of Tums one day, and I remembered the saying: "Tums for the tummy." Before I started the drive home, I put one of the tablets in my mouth and let it dissolve on my tongue. It was like a miracle that my stomach started to feel better. So I took another one. I considered that pain a wakeup call for me to pay more attention to my own physical needs, as I provided leadership for this event the students had looked forward to all year.

They chose the theme music of the television show, "Love Boat," for background music for the student-models to present their garments. Ebony fashion models taught them how to model and do quarter, half, and full turns for the second year. I wrote up a description of the style of the garment, the fabric, and the name and year of each student. I watched their beaming faces, detecting a combination of pride and fear, happiness and nervousness. Some of the girls had a flair for showing off their garments. On the other extreme were those who had to overcome shyness, but joined in the fun like everyone else, because they wanted to be part of this first-ever fashion show at Waller High School. We had a balanced racial and ethnic mix of students working together on the common goal of giving the fashion show and they got to share their unique gifts and talents. Some were preparing to serve refreshments; some were doing publicity and invitations; and some worked with the staging. I felt a sense of accomplishment, proof to myself that I must have treated all ethnic groups fairly and equally, because all races and nationalities wanted to be in the club and the after-school program. Beverly, the bridge! Beverly, the Peacemaker! I was genuinely happy.

When I arrived home from school on May 4, 1970, the television news was that four Kent State University students were shot and killed by the Ohio National Guard. Many others were injured. My stomach turned over. I felt sick. How could this be?

The first news accounts were that Ohio National Guard soldiers fired live ammunition into a crowd of Kent State student protesters. Four students were killed, four were seriously wounded, and many more injured. I thought, *Oh, my gosh, now the National Guard has brought the war home. What is this world coming to?*

The events leading up to this calamity were that on April 30, President Nixon announced on television that as Commander in Chief, he had given orders for military air raids to hit enemy troop concentrations in Cambodia and for troops to do cross-border action into Laos to stop movement of supplies along the Ho Chi Minh Trail. EJ hadn't been stationed too far away from the Ho Chi Minh Trail. I wondered how the war was now affecting all the work that he did with the Laotian people. Weird as it may seem, the very next day happened to be May first, the traditional day for celebrating freedom movements. Instead of freedom, student pro-testers woke up to news of the new war initiative. The official line was still that the Vietnam War was winding down, but all could see that it was actually escalating and now involved two more coun-tries—Laos and Cambodia. Passionate and angry demonstrations erupted on college campuses all over the United States.

Kent State college officials called on the Ohio National Guard to help local police try to control the expanding numbers of angry protesters. Guardsmen threw canisters of tear gas into the groups of protesters. Some college students apparently picked them up and threw them back at the guardsmen. In the confusion some guardsmen heard an order to shoot. Some shot in the air. Some shot straight into the crowd of demonstrators. Four young lives were extinguished. Four idealistic minds and voices silenced for-ever. Hundreds of young people had trusted they had the right to exercise their freedom to protest the war without being attacked and killed. It was the final loss of innocent trust in the government and the birth of cynicism. Kent State students and students every-where became possibly the most tragic casualties of peacemaking during the Vietnam War.

I realized that almost all the antiwar and protest activities in which my friends and I participated had that kind of potential for vio-lence. Was peacemaking worth the risk?

The risk is great. Protesting unjust wars and unjust laws pits peacemakers up against those in power who are invested in the status quo, who do not question the powers and principalities, and whose job it is to maintain order. When their authority is defied, they are trained to respond with force or with weapons, if ordered. They are not trained nor do they have the time to listen and reason with other people. Last but not least, the biggest tragedy is that there are obviously evil persons in power, who think they can eliminate the vision of a peaceable world if they eliminate leaders with the vision.

On the other hand, young adult protesters need to understand the purpose of a demonstration. There are limits. It is only to try to get attention for their cause and win people over. Decisions about war and peace are made at a different level in a different venue. Young war protesters standing up against young armed military men can add up to a volatile situation with no room for compromise. Young policemen and young national guardsmen are probably no more mature than young protesters. Everyone's life may depend upon each side putting themselves in the shoes of those against whom they are positioned. Nonviolence requires discipline in the same way as military duty requires discipline. Neither military duty nor peacemaking is for the faint of heart. But military folks and policemen have the weapons, which means they are more dangerous and ultimately have more responsibility.

The "Kent State Massacre" seemingly ended the massive college student protest movement. However, Kent State student sacrifices must have motivated President Nixon and Secretary of State Henry Kissinger finally to take bolder steps to end the war without escalating it further. It wasn't long after that they started talking of "peace with honor," which they would accomplish by:

1. "Vietnamization" or training of war troops and leadership
2. Reduction of casualties of war
3. Gradual withdrawal of US troops
4. Beginning Paris Peace Talks in order to negotiate settlement of the war

Unintended consequences of the war included:

1. Drug abuse was becoming a problem among soldiers, blamed on declining morale fighting a long war which seemed increasingly more unwinnable
2. Prisoners-of-war were being identified and soldiers lost in action counted and identified

There was one happy news item: the Marine Corps was the first to announce they would no longer accept draftees. They would re-institute voluntary enlistments.

Is peacemaking worth the risk? My answer was still yes, but it must be done peacefully or it is not peacemaking. I will still demonstrate, but I will never go out of my way to antagonize the police or military. They have their job to do. Our goal is to win over the minds and hearts of the people of the world, to keep alive the vision of a world of peace with justice.

Graduation day! June 13, 1970. I blinked my eyes and looked twice at the graduation program. My name, Beverly Kae Johnson, was incredibly there right in the middle of a long list of candidates for Masters of Arts degrees. My parents who traveled in from Iowa took pictures with me in my cap and gown, and we chatted while we waited to line up for the outdoor ceremony at the Northwestern University football stadium. They said they were proud of me for my accomplishments and how I overcame many obstacles in order to earn this advanced degree. I couldn't even think what obstacles they were talking about other than rheumatic fever. They reminded me that while a full-time student from 1965 to 1967, I worked three part-time jobs as an adult education sewing instructor in two community centers in Chicago and a wedding organist for the chapel at Garrett/Northwestern. When I was running out of money, I didn't ask them—I took almost a year off to work in two dietetics departments, first Presbyterian-Saint Luke's Hospital, then Michael Reese Hospital, and finally returned to Garrett/Northwestern to complete my final quarter of classes in the spring of 1968. The next year, I presented written and oral final exams while I worked as a first-year teacher. My parents told me I should feel genuinely happy that I didn't give up and I finished what I started.

For my graduation present, they were not going to make me finish paying back the car I got from my brother Erwin. The car was now named Tough Buddy, the famous black and white Ford Fairlane 300 that started this whole saga. There was one condition—I was to use the money I would have paid them to make a trip to Germany with Rachel to visit family relatives. That sounded good to me.

After the ceremony I showed my parents where I lived on campus when I was a student, where I lived next door to Wrigley Field, and where I worked at Waller High School. They said they never liked Chicago, but they could tell I loved the big city. I sang a line from the popular song "Different strokes for different folks," feeling very independent with my own likes and dislikes, no need to justify them or convince my parents of anything. That evening we had a spontaneous celebration in the apartment—my mother, my father, Rachel, Markie, roommate Janice, and me.

I taught them words to a song I had written, sung to the theme song of Reverend Neuman's favorite movie, *Zorba the Greek*. Everyone except my dad got up and danced around the apartment, singing at the top of our lungs:

> *Christ is life and*
> *life is joy and*
> *joy is love and*
> *love is here and*
>
> *(repeat twice)*
>
> *and Christ is life and joy and love.*
> *May He bring life and joy and love this summer!*

My parents told us that evening how they were surprised that so many races and nationalities were so friendly with one another. They said that in that one day, they had said hello to blacks, whites, Hispanics, and Asians at the college and also in the north side neighborhoods in which we lived and worked. I told them I had an intuition that race relations would be a major issue during my lifetime, and I was prepared to be on the helpful side.

The folks asked what happened to the student protesters who were in college or grad school in the last half of the 1960s like I was. They had half expected to see a demonstration since that generation was graduating with me—after all, the Vietnam War was still raging on and official peace talks were painfully slow. They asked what was going to happen to the youthful idealism after we all graduated and started careers. I said young people had to work in order to eat and live just like everyone else, but maybe they would still change the world in ways no one could predict.

It did seem to be true that the antiwar movement had already petered out, at least in the Midwest, after the Conspiracy Seven trial and the Kent State student massacre. It gave me a hollow feeling as though something supremely important was being allowed to die. I knew a lot of demonstrators probably wanted the war to end while they were in college, and when it didn't happen, they got discouraged or cynical and gave up. What was being allowed to die was the empowerment when groups of diverse peoples come together to accomplish something bigger than one person could do alone. I told my folks I felt I was "by my lonesome" now, but I was going to keep looking for a group of active peacemakers on a mission.

The next day was Sunday. My folks, my sister, my nephew, and I went to Humboldt Park United Methodist Church together. Reverend Jim Neuman preached an inspired sermon entitled "You Are Accepted," based on a sermon by a famous theologian named Paul Tillich. We talked enthusiastically about that sermon over dinner. We agreed we all were important to God, and there wasn't one part of our diverse and fragmented lives that Jesus did not care about. As we waved good-byes, I realized with a jolt that it was not up to me to hold everything together. Jesus Christ our Savior holds everything together, and we get to see glimpses of Christ's vision for a peaceable world from time to time as we go through life doing the best we can. It is Christ's vision that will come to pass. As a peacemaker, I could forget striving alone; I was part of Christ's perfect vision!

That summer I put into practice my hard-learned lessons about overwork. My only work was on lesson plans for the new class I would be teaching, Personality Development-Family Living, that next fall, in addition to Clothing and Foods and Nutrition. I was starting to take control of my life by not working any job during "summer vacation," which meant using money management skills to make my ten-month salary last until school started again.

Because I was determined to enjoy the city I lived in, I attended free Grant Park concerts and other outdoor events Chicago had to offer. I went to Chicago Cubs baseball games every free Ladies' Tuesday home game. Watching the men hawking hot dogs, beer, and soda pop for what seemed like outrageous prices, I got a bright idea for my after school club. We could sell hot dogs and soda pop at the home basketball games, and the money we made could be used for a big field trip at the end of next school year such as to Saint Louis Great America. I just knew the students in my after-school club would like that idea and I hoped so would the school administration.

I started attending singles' group activities with Janice at the downtown Fourth Presbyterian Church. A huge number of people my age attended, because the programs were on topics that were important to young adults my age, such as healthy relationship building, modern music, the Vietnam war, finding our place in the world by identifying our calling, money management, and much more. The pastor in charge worked with group leaders to create a welcoming climate for emerging, struggling, young people to "find themselves" regarding lifestyles, wants and desires, ambitions, and persistent problems. There was plenty of time for socializing, and we were invited but not required to attend the Sunday evening wor-ship. I liked being in groups of guys and gals, not feeling required to pair off, like when I was in high school and college. Without the need to choose or decline offers, I could just listen to guys talk and get to know how they think and feel, a new experience for me. It didn't bother me that I wasn't dating anyone special. I was finally learning things I needed to know about that enigmatic other sex.

Counseling sessions continued to be hard work and that summer I wrote extensively in my journal. One day I was inspired to write the following:

Who I Am and Who I Want to Be

Someone with a vision that all people might reach their personal fulfillment

Someone who treasures happiness

Someone who seeks adventure in ordinary life

Someone who really cares for others

Someone who craves love, even though I won't ask for it. Sometime I will.

Someone who wants to be part of real life, to see things as they really are

Someone who is not afraid to feel despair, pain, alienation

Someone who has the courage to act on important issues

Someone who gives my life to the service of those around me, and yet—

Someone who will no longer be abused, used, or disrespected

Someone not afraid to be different when it is good to be so

Someone truly loving God and dedicated to Him and His will (regardless of outward appearances)

Someone who will share this life with all human beings, in all the ways I can, in all the places I can, and in all the times I can, and add a little something to each person's life that I touch from now on

Someone who loves life and treasures it.

My counselor commented on this writing, saying, "It sounds like you are crossing a new threshold—to a life of healthy relationships. You are leaving the mission field for good."

✳

My counselor and I spent some time revisiting and reflecting on my three months of rest and recuperation. I realized it gave me a chance to get my mind around some deeper life truths that had been obscured by the hustle and bustle of daily activities. One paradox was that although I was quite sick, I never felt bad and I never feared that I would not get better. I began to pay more attention to my body and spirit connection, and I made a wonderful discovery—there is healing energy in the midst of illness. Eventually the healing was able to take over and my rest and recuperation time was completed. I thought I had become a more philosophical person in those months.

Life was not so simple for me anymore. For instance, I lost my limited view of the world and the people in it whom I had categorized as right or wrong, good or bad, with nothing in between. I developed a new visualization of living in this world as a bell curve. On one end is the totally perfect way and on the opposite end is the totally deprived, evil, wrong-headed way. In-between is reality-based living with all its complexity. That was where I wanted to be present to myself and the world. I loved the beauty of life—its curves and waves, its surprises and miracles, its paradoxes, its ups and downs with periods of sadness and joy all mixed together.

I believe I became more "laid back," less intense on the need to capture all of life's experiences all at once. Most of the events of life are way beyond my control. Even after all the antiwar protesting and sacrifices, the war still marched on. As hard as I had worked to become independent, I was dependent on others to help me through my recuperation. As much as I craved a new love relationship, I had none at the present time. And that was okay.

The time would come. I knew how I had declined marriage many times since my high school years. I knew that most of my friends married right after high school or right after college, and my field of possibilities was much smaller than before. However, my counselor brought up an interesting thought: I might start looking for guys who were divorced or widowed, rather than single guys. Guys who were married once might not have all the hang-ups, which protect themselves from close relationships.

I began to wonder about the seeming silence of the church during the student war protest movement and to question whether or not our church denomination even had a stand on war and peace. I asked our church pastor and he referred me to the Social Principles in the Discipline of the now United Methodist Church. I took a cursory look and found no clear-cut statements, so I asked the pastor if our church could do a study on why the church should be against war. He approved under two conditions: one, we would take an open-ended questioning approach on war and peace, and two, I would be willing to lead the study group. He helped me formulate the invitation as a question: Are you interested in exploring the relationship between war and Christianity in light of the current war in Vietnam? The goal of the study would be to answer two questions: As a Christian, how do I feel about the Vietnam War? What can we as a church do about it?

Only six other church members signed up, ages eighteen to eighty, all women. We started out by sharing why we were interested in the topic. Most of them knew someone who was serving in the war. Then we decided we had better learn some facts about the current progress of the war. Although President Nixon and National Security Advisor Henry Kissinger had set the objective to end the Vietnam War by bringing "peace with honour," in actuality 1969 ended up being called "the bloodiest year yet." President Nixon began US troop withdrawals while national defense was to be passed over to the South Vietnamese, but by the end of the year, there were still 349,700 troops in South Vietnam.

It was being predicted that the Vietnam War would end up being America's longest war. It would last from 1963 to 1975. More than 2.7 million American men would serve in South Vietnam before the war was over and 3.7 million in the Vietnam theatre of war, including Thailand, Guam, the Philippines, and the South China Sea. Three out of four young American men would wear our country's uniform in military service, the average age 19.2 years old. The tour of duty was one year, but many soldiers were redeployed. (Steinman, Ron. *The Soldiers' Story: Vietnam in Their Own Words.* New York: Fall River Press, 1999; and Daugherty, Leo. *The Vietnam War Day by Day.* NY: Chartwell Books, 2011.)

There would be 58,213 American casualties of war by the end of the Vietnam conflict. Three out of four of them were under age 23. Our group couldn't recall reading in the newspaper about any hometown soldier returning dead or alive, and no one heralded as a war hero on television. There seemed to be official silence on the consequences of war. Due to the controversy regarding the war, returning soldiers remained quiet about their time in Vietnam. The "silent generation" soldiers had to be bearing their grief and horrible memories silently. The only good news was that when guys returned, the economy was strong enough that most were able to get jobs or return to their old jobs.

We found some surprises in the church discipline and official statements on war and peace. We discovered our church was not a pacifist church, because it allowed war as a last resort.

We learned about "just criteria for war" attributed originally to Saint Augustine:

- It must follow the prior use of all means of reconciliation.
- It must have clearly stated just goals.
- It must employ the least possible amount of killing and deadly violence.
- It must be as brief as possible.
- It must have a clearly thought-out strategy for ending the war.
- Reparations must be made following the end of the war.

Our further investigation into the literature revealed "just war theory" actually harked back to Aristotle and had the following criteria: just cause, just intent, last resort, legitimate authority, reasonable hope of success, discrimination, and proportionality.

Our little group decided that the Vietnam conflict did not meet any of those criteria. It did not qualify as a just war. It was the opposite of a just war. We felt the only wars fought by the United States which met the just war criteria were the Second World War and the Civil War.

A new church member joined our class one day. He said he was a Vietnam veteran and he just wanted to listen. When the meeting time was almost over, he spoke with a quiet, halting voice.

"You've been studying whether there should be war or not. This is hard for me to put into words, but I have a question." With sad, almost desperate eyes, he continued with a trembling voice. "One of the Ten Commandments is, do not kill, right? I need to know, how can I keep on living with myself, with what I did in Vietnam? I sinned and sinned bad." He lowered his head almost to his knees and just sat there. I was stunned, not knowing what to say. The rest of the group was silent, too, until the oldest lady in our group spoke with a kind voice.

"My dear friend, you were in a war. You did what you had to do."

"No, it's more complicated than that. I just know I didn't do the right thing. That's all I can say about it. I need to know, is there any hope for me?" He looked straight at me with pleading eyes.

My voice stumbled. "Are you asking—can there be forgiveness for you? Does God forgive even the worst of sins?"

He nodded. The oldest lady immediately spoke with authority. "Yes, he can and he does! Believe me, that's what God did when his son, Jesus, died on the cross. He forgave our sins, all of them, and God forgives you, my friend. You too are forgiven like everyone who is truly sorry for his sins."

"Oh, God, I hope that's true." His voice was a rough whisper.

We all said together "It is."

I wished afterwards we had prayed with him as a group, but he seemed relieved. I think our discussion and acceptance of him was all the prayer that was needed. That was the only meeting our Vietnam veteran friend attended and he didn't attend church regularly. I could only hope it was healing for him. He had introduced us to the personal collateral damage, which is forced on all soldiers who serve our country during wartime.

At the next meeting, we began to study what the church needs to do about war. Someone brought two sermons by H. Richard Niebuhr, "War as the Judgment of God" preached on May 13, 1942 and "War as Crucifixion" preached on April 28, 1943 in the context of the Second World War.

All the Christian groups seem to be resolved to exert all their powers to affect a just peace settlement—a peace which will not be based on the interpretation that only one nation is being judged or that the victors are the judges, but rather on the knowledge that all nations have fallen short of simple justice, not to speak of the glory of God.

We as a group felt humbled as we came to the realization that all of us have participated in the Vietnam war whether through action or inaction; therefore, we as Christians all need to ask God's forgiveness for this war and all our nations' wars "in reliance on the continued grace of God in the midst of our ungraciousness." (In *War as Crucifixion: essays on peace, violence and 'just war.* Chicago: Christian Century Press, 2002)

At the end of the six-week study period, our group garnered a consensus. We were against war under any circumstance, unless absolutely everything else had been tried and failed. We took an action which seemed totally inadequate, but at least we took a public stand against the war. We wrote the following letter and sent it to President Nixon:

Dear President Nixon:

In our church we are studying just war and the pacifist stances toward war. We feel that the USA has a tremendous responsibility and opportunity to make a Christian witness to the entire world, surprising everyone by not continuing the ways of the world in which all governments do war, but as a "nation under God" taking the challenge of the Bible seriously and creating a new value system in the world in which our country will pursue peace most aggressively and creatively.

Sincerely,
Humboldt Park United Methodist Church
study group members

We never heard back. I guess it was too little too late for the leaders of our country. But the letter was not returned, so I felt we had been heard by someone on his staff. The pastor published our letter in the church newsletter. It was well received by our congregation but we never heard from anyone in the church hierarchy either. Working through the system had advantages, but getting decision-makers to listen to us wasn't one of them.

I told my brother, EJ, about our class. He said he was worried about what would happen to the thousands of Laotian and Vietnamese people who had sided with the United States of America if and when we pulled out. He had written letters to Nixon, too, about his concerns for those who would need protection from the conquerors. Would America provide for them to immigrate to America? But once they arrived here, would they still be in trouble unless they had a sponsor who cared enough to continue to help them and their families? He told me he was working with our rural church in Iowa to sponsor such a family from Vietnam.

I listened to a lot of music, paying special attention to war protest songs.

"War! What is it good for?
Absolutely nothing.
Say it again, y'all!"

"Where have all the soldiers gone? Long time passing.
Gone to graveyards everyone."

Joan Baez wrote and performed popular antiwar music such as *The Green, Green Grass of Home.* Pete Seeger wrote and sang *Waist Deep in the Big Muddy* and many more. The Kingston Trio brought Pete Seeger's antiwar songs into the mainstream. Pat Paulson declared himself a candidate for president with one item on his platform—to abolish the draft. The Smothers Brothers, Tommy and Dicky, helped young people find something to laugh about regarding the politics surrounding the war. With these big names, the antiwar movement finally was gaining legitimacy through-out the country. "War no more" became a motto bringing more and more folks together. Perfect strangers could flash the peace symbol and understand each other. Ending the war was becoming a national goal.

✴

One day I read a little blurb in the newspaper about six veterans who had marched together in a 1967 peace demonstration and had just started a new organization, Vietnam Veterans against the War. I thought, *What if I started a new organization, Former War Protesters still against War? I would have to write a position paper or an invitation to encourage people to join.*

I started making a list of random thoughts to develop:

1. Here I am, thirty-one years old. My life is framed by wars. Born during the final build-up to the Second World War, going to school during the Korean War, and moving to Chicago during the Vietnam War, I have never really experienced a world at peace. Soldiers and citizens alike have never had time to find closure and forgiveness for the casualties of one war before they and their children are thrust into another war. So many veterans were living with war wounds—physical, mental, emotional, and spiritual. So many families continuing in spite of their losses and casualties, everyone longing for peace.

2. I am becoming focused on the acts of war against war pro-testers and peacemakers here at home in the United States of America. I am making a list of casualties of peacemaking, starting with the one I knew personally, the Reverend Bruce Johnson (1969), who was carrying out his vision and mission to transform youth gang leadership and encouraged preven-tion through Mayor Daley's Peace Corps Program.

3. Former President John F. Kennedy (1963) inspired our gen-
    eration to join Peace Corps, when he said, "Ask not what your
    country can do for you; ask what you can do for your country."
    He had been making agreements about a phased withdrawal
    from Vietnam shortly before his assassination. (Richard
    Reeves. *President Kennedy: Profile of Power.* New York: Simon
    & Schuster, 1993.)

4. Bobbie Kennedy (1968) was running for the Democratic
    nomination to follow in his brother's footsteps.

5. The Reverend Martin Luther King, Jr. (1968) was following
    his extremely dangerous calling to transform America into a
    place in which all could live in equality and justice. He had
    just begun preaching against the unjust Vietnam War before
    he was assassinated. (Dyson, Michael Eric. *April 4, 1968:
    Martin Luther King Jr's Death and How It Changed America.*
    Philadelphia: Basic Civitas Books, 2008.)

6. Malcolm X (1965), charismatic leader, spoke against the war.

7. Fred Hampton and Mark Clark (1969), charismatic leaders,
    were attracting many followers.

8. The four antiwar demonstrators at Kent State (1970) who were
    killed have to be counted.

9. There were still lynchings in the South as well as cross burn-
    ings and Ku Klux Klan rallies. I decided to start collecting
    names and stories of casualties going back to the fifties when
    I first became sensitized along with many other college stu-
    dents in the nation. In Chicago we knew about Emmet Till,
    a fourteen-year-old Chicagoan who was condemned to death
    by the KKK while visiting relatives in Mississippi for whistling
    at a white woman, just like my walks past construction sites in
    downtown Chicago, an annoyance, but hardly a fatal crime.

10. Edward Aaron, was a young man kidnapped and killed by
    Klansmen in Birmingham, Alabama, for something similar to
    what Emmet Till did innocently.

11. George W. Lee, a black minister, was one of the first blacks who openly registered blacks to vote in Mississippi; he was shot and killed.

12. That didn't stop Lamar Smith, a black voting rights activist, to continue to register blacks to vote right outside a Mississippi courthouse, but a bullet did.

13. Medgar Evers, a civil rights activist in Mississippi, was one of the rash of killings in 1963. There were also seven killings in Birmingham, Alabama that year.

14. School integration was a pretext for many more killings. Student Virgil Ware, age 13, was killed by two white youths, and Johnny Robinson, age 16, was killed by police.

15. Four little school girls just starting school were killed by a bomb in 1963. Their names were Denise McNair, Addie Mae Collins, Carole last name anonymous, and Cynthia Diane Wesley. (McKinstry, Carolyn Maull. *While the World / Watched: A Birmingham Bombing Survivor Comes of Age during the Civil Rights Movement.* Tyndale House Publishers, 2011.) When children in school became the fatal victims of racial hatred and prejudice, it was a tipping point for Americans throughout the nation. The Civil Rights Act of 1964 soon came to pass.

16. Jonathan Myrick Daniels, an Episcopal seminary student from New Hampshire, answered Reverend King's call in 1965 to join civil rights workers in the South. He stepped in front of a shotgun blast meant for another worker in Haynesville, Alabama. The person whose life he saved was Ruby Sales, who later became founder and director of SpiritHouse, an Atlanta-based nonprofit project dealing with discrimination. She said, "Race relations today in the United States are an extension of that time period."

17. Last but not least in my experience was Eugenia Johnson, the pastor's wife, killed when Bruce was killed.

I know there are many more. Were there casualties overseas among volunteers during the early years of President Kennedy's Peace Corps Program? I didn't know. Casualties of peacemaking were not counted by the government the way casualties of war were counted. How long was this going to continue here in the United States of America?

One day toward summer's end I was walking down State Street in Chicago's Loop when I noticed a number of people hawking daily newspapers for a dime. The general circulation newspapers were featuring stories of young white people burning draft cards, flags, and bras in protest of the war and women's second-class status. I studied my reflection as I walked along, and wondered, what would I look like not wearing a bra? I always wore a 32A bra and a girdle to keep any part of my bust or behind from moving visibly. I wondered what it would be like to dress more freely—not that I wanted to burn my bra, but maybe I could start leaving my girdle at home. I particularly disliked wearing it everywhere I went.

Suddenly a young black man approached me offering a newspaper for a quarter. He said, "News from the streets of California." He was dressed in the Black Panther uniform—a black beret, creased black slacks, a black leather jacket, a starched powder blue shirt, and a black tie. I bought one out of curiosity, thinking it might have some news about how Bobby Seale was doing those days.

The cover article was indeed about Huey Newton and Bobby Seale being arrested for blocking the sidewalk at the Sacramento state capitol while giving a speech. In Newton's speech he had pointed out that blacks were being drafted into the service at a much higher rate than whites. Fifty percent of those Californians drafted and sent to Vietnam were black, much higher percent-age than blacks in the general population. He stated that blacks were also arrested and jailed in higher numbers than whites. He called for his brothers and sisters to revolt and rebel against the racist system. The money gained from selling newspapers would go toward financial resources needed to bail the brothers and sis-ters out of jail and give legal aid "to righteously defend themselves against racists." (Seale Bobby. *A Lonely Rage: The Autobiography of Bobby Seale*. New York: Times Books, 1978.)

The Black Panther Party for Self-Defense first began by train-ing twenty men who wanted to join them in their efforts—Bobby Seale taught Malcolm X philosophy and Huey Newton taught law. They drew up a ten-point platform which aligned their action plan with California laws and programs. Members would carry arms; they would patrol the police as witnesses as they made arrests; their very presence would help prevent police brutality; all self-defense activities would be strictly legal; they would print their own newspapers so as to convey their message accurately.

I wondered what it would be like if every young person were required to do two years of service to their country, their com-munity, or their church? I was just one person who had experi-enced how lives were changed for the better by Mayor Daley's Peace Corps, by President Kennedy's Peace Corps, by the Quakers International Voluntary Service (IVS), by the Methodist Church short-term mission program, by young teachers teaching in poor, neglected, and isolated neighborhoods, by health care workers in the same neighborhoods, and of course by military service.

CHAPTER 12
Rebuilding

FALL, 1970

It was the Tuesday after Labor Day and I was genuinely excited to begin my third year of teaching. It felt so good to be healthy. I never appreciated good health and abundant energy so much before. On the first day of school a student in my clothing class approached me about becoming the school sponsor for a group of students learning West African dances. They wanted to make their African dashiki costumes in the after-school program. Of course, I said yes, delighted that they would choose me for their sponsor. I knew then that I had met my private goal to learn to relate to black students as well as white, Hispanic, and Asian students.

I loved my choice of work—teaching home economics to inner-city kids. Each school day's established routine was order in motion, with lots of noise, plenty of responsibilities, and daily surprises. I was always fine-tuning my "policeman role" as I maintained a state of readiness for unexpected misbehavior. Yet I kept the balance I learned from Bruce—students working on the lessons of the day, but with freedom to follow their own interests and develop their skills.

Textiles and Clothing and Foods and Nutrition classes were the same as last year, but with the new assignment from the Board of Education that *all teachers are teachers of reading and math*. I applied more reading assignments with comprehension exercises and included discussion in my curriculum plans. I also integrated mathematics, such as doubling recipes and converting them to serve a different number of people. Home Economics was amenable to teaching practical applications of math and reading comprehension.

My new class, Personality Development and Family Living, was not a lab class, but it rapidly became my favorite. I could incorporate all kinds of thinking skills and problem-solving, imagining different endings to life problems depending on choices made. I found boys liked to work as individuals and girls preferred to work in small groups. So I also encouraged each gender to work in the opposite mode – boys in groups to develop honest, straightforward communication skills and girls to think for themselves and present their ideas with authority. Sex education was part of this class, too. I was surprised how little the students knew about the biology of the reproductive systems, but how intense was their interest and ability to made healthy decisions when thinking them through ahead of time. I discovered a good resource book *Our Bodies, Ourselves* which was not for students but it de-sensitized me to talking about sexuality and I myself learned a lot from that teacher resource book especially about birth control.

I found myself appreciating the change of pace in the after school program even more than before. I enjoyed helping the girls in the African dance group design and construct their dashiki dance costumes. I sometimes took pictures in my mind and labeled them *the peaceable world* when black, white, Hispanic, and Asian girls were getting to know each other, chatting, and working on different projects to improve their homes and their families and their own lives and their communities.

Different strokes for different folks
So on and so on, a doobee doobee do
We gotta live together.
There is a yellow one that won't accept the black one
That won't accept the green one that won't accept the white one
Different strokes for different folks.

My mind soared like a bird when I discovered that hardly any of the students in the after-school program had ever been outside the city of Chicago; many of them had never even traveled downtown to the Chicago Loop. I planned field trips to the Art Institute to view paintings and fashion, and also I hoped to take a busload of girls to the international food exposition at McCormick place. I thought, *Wouldn't it be wonderful if I could get permission to take the girls on an extended field trip to Iowa to see first-hand where food comes from and to experience the rural way of life on a family farm? That would really be a cross-cultural experience.* I smiled, thinking of the endless possibilities for expanding the girls' worlds as my own world was expanding by living and working in Chicago. Two years later, I would be able to arrange that field trip to Iowa, and the girls would stay in the homes of Iowa friends and neighbors who belonged to the Young Mothers Club. Yoshiko, my sister-in-law, was active in that group and Miye Sumita, a teacher's aide who went as a chaperone, stayed with EJ and YJ.

My formal request to the school administration resulted in permission for the after-school club to sell hot dogs and soda pop during the half-time break of home basketball games. Because we gave one free hot dog and one glass of soda pop to each basketball player, the girls loved to work with the club. It was a perfect chance for them to meet the varsity basketball players. The school policeman recommended me for crowd control pay for after my pay for the tenth period after-school program ended. So after clean-up, I went into the second half of the games when more crowd control staff was needed. I got to know the coaches better and eventually my teacher intern invited them to come into the home economics/foods room for lunch periods. This teacher intern, the first student from Chicago State College assigned to me as a student teacher for one semester, was creative using the left-over food ingredients to make hot lunch dishes that coaches and Home Ec teachers liked. One of the coaches took me for a spin in his gorgeous shiny black Cadillac and told me he was impressed by how much I knew about cars and sports. Just as the students loved meeting basketball players, I liked meeting the coaches.

At home I started getting up a half hour earlier than I needed to eat breakfast and ready myself for work. I made coffee and sat in the front room where I could look out the window at the trees and sky in the direction of Lake Michigan. It was quiet at five-thirty in the morning! I loved the peace and quiet of the early morning city with birds singing and commuter trains rattling down the elevated train tracks somewhere nearby. I came to depend on this time to get my mind focused on the needs and possibilities of the current day in front of me. I could also ponder some of my life's questions, such as where did I see and experience love around me.

My mother and I settled into a routine of having phone conversations every couple weeks. One day I said, "Mom, there's talk in my school about planning to celebrate Martin Luther King's birthday in February along with the birthdays of Presidents Washington and Lincoln."

"Oh, really? Why, I wonder?"

"Because he's a modern-day hero. They say kids need to know more about what he stood for, instead of thinking about rioting in April on the day he was assassinated. It would be more productive to have teenagers read his speeches in February, the month he was born. Martin Luther King provided many teachable moments like 'I have a dream' which provides a hopeful vision for a better America."

"I didn't realize his speeches were so educational."

"Actually I didn't either until I started reading some of them."

"Didn't you say you went to hear him speak in person?"

"Yes. The talk I heard wasn't very educational; it was more personal. My friend Anna Mae and I went to hear him when he came to Chicago to march for civil rights in Cicero (an all-white working class suburb bordering on Chicago.) Somehow the march had been prevented or curtailed. He really looked beaten down and extremely disappointed on the stage that night."

"Isn't he a Baptist preacher? What did he speak about?"

"I actually found part of the text of that speech. Listen to this. He said, 'I have no martyr complex. I want to live as long as anybody in this building tonight, and sometimes I begin to doubt whether I'm going to make it through. I must confess I'm tired.'" I paused, but Mom didn't say anything, so I continued, "'I don't mind saying to Chicago or anybody ... I'm tired of marching for something that should have been mine at birth. I don't mind saying this to you this night ... I'm tired of the tensions surrounding the days. I don't mind saying to you tonight ... that I'm tired of living every day under the threat of death. ... Yes. I'm tired of going to jail; I'm tired of all of the surging murmur of life's restless sea.' " (Dyson, Michael Eric. *April 4, 1968: Martin Luther King Jr's Death and How It Changed America*. Philadelphia: Basic Civitas Books, 2008.)

Remembering the speech that Mom left out at home for me to read, I asked, "You don't still think he was a communist, do you, Mom?"

"Well, I guess I'm unsure now. J. Edgar Hoover says that's why there was so much violence at his marches. Communists cause violence, you know, because they want to break up America from within, to destroy our freedom and our way of life."

"Yeah, yeah. But Martin Luther King's most famous speech was 'I have a dream—that one day people will be judged by the content of their character and not the color of their skin.' That doesn't sound like someone trying to destroy America to me. That sounds like someone trying to build up America, to make us better."

"That's true, but actions speak louder than words."

I hesitated a moment. "That's a good point. Other Black leaders might be out there promoting violence, but Reverend King never once did. He insisted on nonviolence. His marchers themselves were never violent, Mom."

"But he marched where he wasn't wanted. He knew it would cause violence."

"Did he?" I was starting to get riled up, so I took a deep breath and continued carefully. "I think he always marched for a purpose. Remember that time I marched in Des Moines at the Iowa state capital? Nobody invited us to go there to march for open housing. We got a permit, because there's no law against having a march for a purpose. They didn't want us, but they didn't attack us either. (Pause) What's the difference with Reverend King?"

Mom paused. "You're right, Beverly. It couldn't be the peaceful march that caused the violence. Hate causes people to attack peaceful people. Maybe hate and fear."

"Wow, that's an important insight, Mom."

"Maybe the fear comes from things changing too fast."

"Martin Luther King came up north to show us that racial hatred and fear didn't stop at the Mason-Dixon Line. It's in the North, too, in a different way."

"I'm beginning to sense the costs of the civil rights battles for both whites and blacks. When people say he was deliberately fomenting violence, I can see for the first time that he was exercising the rights that any American has in a free country."

"I am, too. Anyway, I wish we could go on longer, but I have to say good night and get my sleep. I really appreciate our conversations, Mom."

"I'm proud of you, Beverly. Good night."

"Good night."

That phone conversation gave me more to ponder. Mom spoke of peacemaking causing violence. It was still hard for me to understand why a peaceful march would consistently foment violence in the South and meet with implacable resistance in the North. One satisfactory answer might be that when there is a social movement in one direction, there will be backlash. Pushing toward change creates discomfort and pressure on the status quo and forces it to change. People who already have all the advantages of life don't like change. At the same time that young people were breaking down racial barriers in the USA, the status quo folks were erecting walls of division and fear.

I remembered when I visited my sister Sydnee in Iowa one weekend, her Lutheran pastor put it this way in this sermon, "Jesus told us to love the poor and the powerless, and now they have our backs against the wall." I wondered if the purpose of his statement was irony or fear. The status quo folks had just come out of the McCarthy era when their biggest passion was to blame communism for everything; they tried to write off civil rights and anti-war activity as anti-Americanism. It wasn't just pitiful, it explained why we went into Vietnam to take over for the French who were tiring of fighting to keep the Communists from spreading their power. The status quo folks had their way and got us into a war in which the cost-benefit ratio gradually became unacceptable to the majority of Americans. The young people bore the biggest part of the cost. It was the youth who were losing our lives. Thinking of protest as a war for justice also helped give me some insight into why civil rights leaders were killed. That was the best I could do to understand the horrific changes happening in America. So much violence. So many deaths. My hope was that our country would eventually become a better place for everyone, not just the privileged.

I asked myself—could the war for civil rights be called a 'just war?' Just wars have just cause, just intents, last resort, legitimate authority, reasonable hope of success, discrimination, and proportionality. Yes, the war for civil rights is the very epitome of just war. But—

"The wheels of justice turn slowly."

—Martin Luther King

✲

One morning during coffee time all the teachers were talking about an after-school course the Board of Education was going to hold on site in Waller High School, because a counselor in our school was the instructor. The course was entitled, "The Civil War and Its Consequences regarding Racial Integration Today." The teachers who were signing up were working toward lane placement salary promotion. I told them that the Board of Education had turned down my application for salary credit for the Master's degree that I earned from Northwestern University/Garrett Seminary because my course of study was about religion. They said I could take a lane placement course anyway; it would count after I got another Master's degree. I signed up.

Our instructor, who was black, immediately took us beyond high school history by challenging our ideas on the motivation for the Civil War—was it to save the union, to free the slaves, or for economic superiority? Through animated discussion we finally saw that all those rationales were at work and the issues were complex. Finally, our instructor painted a picture of a deeply troubled nation in which we were still living with a great deal of unprocessed public pain. The racial turmoil of the 1960s proved that as a nation, we were far from finished with the racial fears and hatred and injustice left behind from the Civil War. War did not solve the problem of a nation attempting to transform itself from one in which a main ingredient of our economic and social systems was legal race-based slavery to a new ideal nation of peoples of all races and nationalities freely working and studying together as equals.

After the Civil War, the nation settled into Jim Crow, which was anything but separate and equal. It was now one hundred years since slavery was abolished. Only in the 1960s had components of and legal strides toward real racial equality been defined, namely the Civil Rights Act of 1964, the Voting Rights Act of 1965, President Johnson's war on poverty, open housing and affirmative action created in 1966, and Title 9 based on Brown vs. Education.

I also took away from this course that we as a nation have yet to acknowledge how our long history of wars are not triumph after triumph, but endless violence, shedding of blood, fallen warriors, destruction, loss of lovely national treasures all over the world, and postponing indefinitely our beloved hopes for peace on earth. Even the Second World War which was often judged as a just war did not finish off anti-Semitism carried to its sinful extreme in the

Holocaust and anti-Japanese prejudice evidenced by relocation/ concentration camps in this country. We hadn't even begun to tap into the horrors of the Vietnam War or tried to heal the divisions laid bare by nation-wide protests and assassinations of the 1960s. Yes, we were a deeply troubled nation with a great deal of unprocessed public pain and we were in need of healing.

Discussions instigated by our course material often focused on Chicago. Most schools were "separate but equal" by necessity, because neighborhoods in Chicago were segregated. In Lincoln Park, the black teachers who worked at Waller High School mostly lived on the South Side and white teachers on the North Side. The black students lived south of Division Avenue, near Cabrini Greens. Asian and Latino teachers who worked at the school and students lived nearby on Armitage Avenue in Lincoln Park and other places on the North Side. I experienced these separate worlds as I continued to do home visits.

Chicago was a city of neighborhoods. Many of them were ethnic-identified, such as Polish, Mexican, Swedish, Italian, Puerto Rican, German, Korean, Chinese, and Bohemian. Some of them were career-identified such as enclaves of artists, steel workers, factory employees, and university employees. Important neighborhoods were identified with parks, the park system originally planned geographically by Daniel Burnham to enhance the quality of life for all of Chicago. The park system was designed to form a large half circle starting and ending at the lakefront, framing and being located about three to five miles from Grant Park in the Chicago Loop: Hyde Park, Jackson Park, Washington Park, Douglas Park, Garfield Park, Humboldt Park, and Lincoln Park. I heard often that there were only seven neighborhoods where mixed couples would be accepted, where more than one race lived together. Otherwise, Chicago was a segregated city exacerbated by economic inequality, which made integrating its seventy-five high schools and five hundred and twenty-five elementary schools problematic.

Chicago neighborhoods were in flux, with the one exception of race. There seemed to be two separate worlds, black and white, and of all things, they seemed to me to be shaped like a cross with a big circle in the middle. The circle around the downtown Loop was given over to low income housing where blacks lived. On Chicago's South Side there was a line along Western Avenue north to south which happened to be the longest street in Chicago. East of the line there were the only two historic black high schools – Phillips and Dunbar. Waller High School on the north side in Lincoln Park was one of the few racially mixed high schools in the city with whites, blacks, Hispanics, and Asians.

The music scene of Chicago was what drew me to neighbor-hoods and downtown, even if I often had to go by myself and ignore implied boundaries. Every year I had a Sunday afternoon subscription to five Chicago Symphony Orchestra concerts. I sat by myself way up in the back of the upper balcony in the "cheap seats," but I could hear just as well as anyone.

One time I decided to go to a much publicized James Brown concert. I had listened to his music on WVON radio and wondered what it would be like to see him in live concert. I just knew that sometime in the future, white people would discover his music and love it like I did. It was raining the day I rode the South Parkway bus, got off, and waited to transfer to the 47th street bus. When it didn't come and didn't come, I was afraid I would be late to the concert, so I raised my umbrella and took off walking east about ten blocks in the rain to the theater. I found myself the only white person in the audience. James Brown himself apparently spotted me, even though I was seated as usual in the back of the theater. In the middle of making some funny remarks, all of the sudden he talked straight at me. I knew he was talking to me, because people around me in the audience turned around and smiled at me. I'm not sure why I didn't understand him, but Brown's jokes seemed to be good-natured, not cruel, so I just smiled.

It reminded me of another time my roommate Janice and I went to the first Operation PUSH convention featuring black-owned businesses. One of us needed to go to the washroom and the other wanted to go on looking at displays. We stood there trying to figure out how we would find each other so we could meet up again. Then all of a sudden we both broke out laughing at the absurdity of not being able to find each other when we were the only two whites there.

Further proof of the two separate worlds of blacks and whites was the existence of two television music and dance showcases— American Bandstand for whites and Soul Train for blacks. I particularly enjoyed listening to WVON, the radio station with black musicians and news. A frequent advertiser, Johnson Publishers, created *Jet Magazine* and *Ebony Magazine*. As a home economics teacher, I attended two affordable gala fashion shows each year – the Ebony Fashion Show and the Presbyterian-St. Luke Hospital Benefit Fashion Show. The terms separate but equal would certainly apply to these art forms and the worlds of entertainment.

The dual goals of true racial equality and voluntary social race relations were just being born in the 1960s. Any attempts were tentative at best, usually embraced by young people, like in our summer program, but not institutionalized. Cultural change was very much still unfinished business. Power shared by the people, all the people, was not reality. Racism was clearly the battle of the century that had affected and would continue to affect almost every citizen and resident of the United States of America. In the 1960s youth looked beyond racist laws and regulations, not ignoring them, not focusing so much on haves and have nots, or on winners and losers, but asking different questions – why can't we just get along and how are we going to relate to each other as equals? Both rules and laws can be changed if there is a willingness to talk to each other, tear down walls, open gates, and build bridges. Instead of looking at confronting racism as the burden of our generation, I chose to look at it as the privilege of our generation.

December 21, 1970

I ran from the kitchen to the front room to catch the telephone as it was ringing incessantly. It was my brother, EJ, laughing and crying at the same time. I sat down, dumbfounded, and listened.

"Hello! Bev! The best thing in the whole world just happened! I'm a father! Our baby is absolutely beautiful! You should see her! She is alive and breathing and wiggling and crying. I have never seen anything like her. Her hands and fingers are so little, just precious! She is our dream come true! Hello. Hello. Are you still there?"

"Of course. Congratulations, father! A baby girl! What wonderful news! How is Yoshiko?"

"She's asleep right now. She's happy, believe me. She worked hard. I feel like I did, too."

"Were you with her when the baby was born?"

"Right up to the minute they took her to the delivery room."

"What's the baby girl's name?"

"Amy Kaiko."

"What?"

"Amy will be her first name. Kaiko her middle name. She's a

true Japanese-American!"

"How about that? Kaiko is almost like my middle name Kae. My first niece! I can hardly wait to see her. But mostly I'm so glad everyone's okay."

"Well, I don't know about me." His laugh was nervous but happy. "Now I'd better hang up and call the rest of the family."

I stood looking out the front window and thought how babies are such a joy and source of hope. Our extended family was growing and we were becoming more international and multi-cultural. First of all, my dad was born in Germany, which actually made my siblings and me first-generation Americans. Then EJ married a Japanese gal and their children will be first-generation Americans as well. I was learning about Japanese culture from Yoshiko as was the community in Iowa through her art work. I often chuckled when I looked at the first picture of her on the farm in Iowa standing by a big mama pig; she was wearing EJ's overalls and holding a pitchfork. She sent it back to her parents in Japan for the shock effect. I thought about how everyone's lives are enriched and made more joyful when we learn and experience other ways of life and beauty. I felt proud that we were a multi-cultural family.

Ever since my friends Reverend Bruce Johnson and Eugenia Johnson had been violently killed and neither the Chicago Police nor the FBI could officially identify the killer, I was looking for pieces to my puzzle called *Why So Many Casualties of Peacemaking*. One day there was a little blurb in the newspaper Nation and World section about a break-in of an FBI office in a suburb of Philadelphia. It was portrayed as just another break-in, like those of recruitment offices to destroy draft records, but I could see this one was different because it was an FBI office. In the time before home computers, it was hard to get more information about anything like this. I had to wait for details to trickle out.

It seems that on March 8, 1971 the whole nation was primed to watch Muhammed Ali's attempt to regain his world heavyweight boxing title against Joe Frazier in Madison Square Garden in New York City. Although I didn't watch it, not being a fan of boxing, certainly most of the sports aficionados in the United States would be watching it, including J. Edgar Hoover and the men of the Federal Bureau of Investigation.

On March 9, a statement was released to Reuters news service from an anonymous source stating that files had been stolen from an FBI office in Pennsylvania by a group that called themselves "Citizen's Commission to Investigate the FBI." They actually broke into an FBI field office on March 8 when everyone was home watching the famous fight. The purpose of this bold act was to get access to secret files, study them, and determine the following:

- "Nature and extent of surveillance and intimidation carried on by the FBI against groups and individuals working for a more just, humane, and peaceful society"

- "How much effort the FBI spent on minor crimes by the poor and powerless for high conviction rates rather than on serious crimes by those with money and influence that cause much damage, i.e. war profiteering, monopolies, institutional racism, organized crime"

- "The extent of illegal practices by the FBI such as eavesdropping, entrapment, and use of provocateurs and informants"

Their statement further spelled out the best summary of the protest movement I had read. "As long as the US government wages war against Indochina in defiance of the vast majority who want all troops and weapons withdrawn this year, and extends that war and suffering under the guise of reducing it; as long as great economic and political power remains concentrated in the hands of a small clique not subject to democratic scrutiny and control, then repression, intimidation, and entrapment are to be expected. We do not believe that this destruction of democracy and democratic society results simply from the evilness, egoism or senility of some leaders. Rather, this destruction is the result of certain social, economic and political institutions."

Just when I feared the nonviolent antiwar movement was becoming defunct, unbeknownst to me at the time, I was wrong. The movement was getting smarter, more focused, and determined to take greater risks for more results. Pennsylvania is far from Chicago but those brave activists gave me answers to my suspicions about killings during the years of my own activism.

Two weeks later the actual files that had been stolen from the FBI offices were sent anonymously to a reporter who worked for the Washington Post by the name of Betty L. Medsger. It came out later what was in the files:

- Case histories obtained secretly by the FBI of thousands of Americans, much malicious gossip about things such as sexual deviance and race mixing, two of J. Edgar Hoover's favorite subjects

- A routine routing slip in 1964 creating COINTELPRO, a huge program of dirty tricks and illegal activities designed to "expose, disrupt, and otherwise neutralize" groups deemed subversive by the director, specifically targeting the Communist Party and the Puerto Rican Independence Party; later additions were Vietnam War activists, the American Indian movement, the women's movement, the New Left, black nationalists (Stokely Carmichael, H. Rap

Brown, Malcolm X, Martin Luther King, Ku Klux Klan, Black Panthers including Breakfast for Children Program and Black Panther newspaper distribution.)

- Memos proving that the FBI enjoyed no government oversight and Hoover committed abuses of power such as persecute King, create a COINTELPRO not subject to US laws, and harass critics of the FBI. COINTELPRO stood simply for Counter-Intelligence-Program.

- Shocking evidence that the Fred Hampton raid in December of 1970 in Chicago was intended to "subvert and eliminate the Black Panther Party and its members." Right in the files, the FBI took credit for his murder and the murder of his colleague Mark Clark, because an FBI informant provided a blueprint of the Black Panthers' Chicago apartment to the Chicago police. The blueprint had a big X on the bed in which Fred Hampton slept and the same on the bed in which Mark Clark slept. Furthermore, after the raid, the FBI installed wiretaps in the phones of the survivors of the raid so that they could listen in on their conversations with their lawyers and subvert the investigation. That was post-raid conspiracy cover up. (Medsger, Betty L. *The Burglary: The Discovery of J. Edgar Hoover's Secret FBI.* New York: Random House, 2014.)

I remembered reading in Chicago newspapers how the Fred Hampton killing was openly carried out by the Chicago police and then investigated by the same Chicago police and the FBI. Their report to the public included an admission that all one hundred gun shot holes came from the outside in; there was a possibility of only one that could have been from the inside out.

J. Edgar Hoover assigned two hundred FBI agents to Pennsylvania to uncover the identity of the burglars, but they never succeeded. He died a year later, never knowing who had illegally broken into one of his offices and uncovered his creation and direct management of the completely illegal and unethical COINTELPRO.

Medsger called the act of breaking into an FBI office "the most powerful single act of nonviolent resistance in American history." She continued her research and finally was able forty years later to get the activists to come forward and be interviewed. Of special interest to me was that when interviewed they identified one of their biggest influences to be Dietrich Bonhoeffer who one activist actually got to know at Union Theological Seminary. They admired his love for his homeland Germany and for his grave personal risk to save that nation, he paid the ultimate price. He was also an inspiration for Martin Luther King. Bonhoeffer himself said he got his understanding of the need for resistance to a government on the wrong course while in Harlem from African Americans and their struggle and willingness to resist. Here was a whole circle of brilliance and passion for justice. I saw it as the church at its best doing the work of Christ in a dangerous world.

Of course, I felt I had been one of the pawns in the FBI game of setting up their case for the Conspiracy Seven trial. I now had a more important question: Were the Bruce and Eugenia Johnson killings only two months before the Fred Hampton and Mark Clark killings in any way due to illegal surveillance of the FBI? Newspaper accounts at the time reported that the FBI and the Chicago Police investigated and never found the one responsible. I knew I was going to have to leave questions like this in the realm of ambiguity. Another counselor, colleague of my counselor, told me, "No one wants you to open that can of worms." I knew there was no way I could do anything about anything here. But I could feel sad about the tremendous number of breaches of both justice and peace against thousands of people. Many lives had been destroyed and what was gained? J. Edgar Hoover never learned that you can't take away people's rights and expect there to be peace. You can't force your wishes on less powerful people and expect there to be peace. You can't get rid of leaders working for justice and expect there to be peace. Peace without justice is not real peace. Somehow in the end, the right will win. The wrong will be exposed and will lose.

CHAPTER 13
Unfinished Business

All these things that happened to me while living through the last two years of the 1960s and first year of the 1970s and were proof of the validity of Martin Luther King Jr's prophetic words just before his death. He said he was no longer afraid, because he'd been to the mountaintop and seen what was in store for our country. It was his vision of all people together, treating each other as equals that gave him determination and courage to continue on the way, and renewed hope in what was to come. I knew I too had caught a glimpse of such vistas, and they inspired me to see this everyday world in which we live through peaceable lenses.

MY NEW YEAR'S RESOLUTIONS

I will study peacemaking and learn to solve crises peacefully. When afraid or angry, I will not respond instinctively and without thinking. Fight or flight might save me, but it will not address a crisis peacefully. The real revolutionary is the one who enters or lives in a typically violent environment, finds a way to be at peace with himself or herself, and makes peace happen around him or her. The peacemaker I want to be is one unafraid to take risks, go against the grain of the status quo, bridge differences, and celebrate harmony.

I will put my resolution into action by creating a unit on peace-making to teach in my Personal Development-Family Living classes, incorporating skills such as problem solving, decision-making, identifying alternative actions, evaluating advantages and disadvantages, empathizing, and caring.

I am full of ideas for the two months of summer vacation I have next summer. I will try to encourage inter-cultural understanding wherever feasible. I will develop and facilitate a cross-cultural language learning activity for my church. (See *Appendix C.*) I will be proactive when I see a public activity or event with one racial group missing, for example, Brookfield Zoo. Janice and I observed only white, Asian, and Latino families enjoying the animals. We called the zoo administration offices and asked them why they didn't advertise on WVON, the radio station that all my students listen to. We did and they did and it worked.

Remembering that summer months are for recreation, literally re-creation, I will act like a true town and country gal. AYH likes members to organize and lead hikes. Starting this summer I am going to plan walking hikes—half day at a county fair and half day at a nearby forest preserve. My first one will be at the Kankakee County Fair, where they have a real live rodeo, and the hike will be at the forest preserve where there is a statue of a Potawatomi Indian chief. If it goes well, I will adapt the same pattern to Kane County, Will County, and Lake County in future summers.

Music will continue to be my passion. As soon as I can save enough money, I am going to buy a Steinway piano, the most expensive one I can afford. I am going to borrow money through the Chicago Teachers' Credit Union and make monthly payments. If I do it right, I will also get a good credit rating, which is better than having no credit rating at all. Then once I have a piano, I can take advanced piano lessons at the American Conservatory of Music. Ruth and Jim Neuman have been urging me to give piano lessons to their girls, Karin, Judi, and Jill. It's hard to believe, but they had a teacher who was so old-fashioned that he hit their hands with a ruler when they made a mistake. My teaching style is probably the polar opposite; I want children to have fun learning and love making music.

Speaking of love, unfortunately there still is no romantic love of my life. I wish there were. I will resolve to look for someone to love and who loves me, patiently taking one step at a time.

1. I will keep on dating, even though they may not be ones to whom I would usually be attracted. I may find out the chemistry takes longer to develop than first impressions. My counselor suggested that I might have to be patient for a few years until the first round of marriages ends for those who got married right out of high school or right out of college. Truthfully, most single guys are fearful of commitment, just like I am. I will keep on working on this in counseling.

2. I will talk to one new person at each social event I attend. This will help me expand my comfort zone. I will listen to them carefully and try to understand their passions and interests.

3. I am going to flirt a little more outrageously, because I know I will eventually "give up my virginity" when I meet the right guy, although I vowed back in church youth group in Iowa to never have sex until marriage. I also vowed never to let liquor touch my lips. At thirty-two years of age now, those particular old never-never rules just couldn't apply forever. But there are new rules for being responsible about sex. I was glad I had read and re-read the book Our Bodies, Ourselves.

My future love life is going to be a little like jazz music. A jazz musician takes what he or she knows of scales, chords, motifs, and melody lines and creates something new. The new creation is in response to some tune, to what other members of the musical group are playing, or even to something random in the environment such as a train whistle. There's an old saying that goes, "There is nothing new under the sun." Maybe it's more like this: we don't throw away old rules completely; we just take them along with our skills and passions and hopes and make new combinations, keeping our essential values and caring about the people in our life, always open to new possibilities. I know love is in my future, hidden in my present.

Last but not least, I intend to travel to see the world. My hope and dream of one day visiting Germany, the homeland of my father and grandparents Carl and Amelia, is beginning to take shape. I knew that both my father and mother had relatives there whom I would love to meet sometime. Also my mother's mother, my grandmother Mabel, spoke Pennsylvania Dutch with her sisters. Mom's father, my grandfather Ralph, spoke Bavarian High German sometimes. My Dad's parents spoke Schleswig-Holstein Low German or *Plot Deutch*. No wonder the world beckons me. I couldn't take German for my foreign language in high school, because it had been cancelled during the Second World War, but I did take Spanish and that opened up many opportunities in my life so far. I will now see if I can learn a third language by taking Conversational German in adult education.

Yes, the world beckons me. (*See last paragraph of Appendix D.*)

APPENDIX A

Questioning the Imponderables

Questions to ponder individually or in group setting:

1. What does peacemaking mean to you? Do you think there are preferable means of promoting peace and what are they?

2. How does providing food play in the efforts of peacemaking? Music?

3. When we read in the Scriptures and the newspapers so much about war and violence, does that mean peacemaking efforts are futile? Why or why not?

4. It is also written in the Scriptures, "Blessed are the peacemakers, for they shall be called the children of God." How does this fit in with the efforts of peacemaking?

5. How do schools and education fit into the picture of peacemaking?

6. Is it possible to overcome cultural differences to provide compatible and peaceful coexistence? Why or why not? How?

7. Peacemaking is definitely risky business, and many have died for this cause. Would you be willing to take that risk? Why or why not?

8. Peace Corps and other such organizations are still active

today. How effective are they? Which organization do you think has made the most impact on world peace?

9. How does media play into peacemaking? Is it helpful or hurtful? Is it truthful enough?

10. Who are some of the greatest peacemakers in history? How have they been effective in the cause?

APPENDIX B

For Those Who Lived Through: Questions About War

One goal of this book is to encourage conversation among those of us born at the end of the silent generation and at the beginning of the baby boomer generation. We remember living through the 1960s, but seldom talk about our experiences. Here are some discussion starters:

1. Where were you during the Vietnam War? Were there any parallels with the people in this book?

2. Is there anything you'd like to bring back from the 1960s?

3. Fifty years ago the Civil Rights Act of 1964 brought great hope for race relations, true equality, and racial harmony. Today the nation is still grappling with feelings, beliefs and prejudices that were born long before any of us. Will we ever quit fighting the Civil War? *— Trump*

4. Is there an "empathy deficit" in our nation? When there is racial turmoil, can you speak convincingly for both sides of the altercation?

5. Do you, as a general rule, seek out both sides of every issue? Are you able to state the case for the other side?

6. Where were you during the 1968 Democratic Convention in Chicago? Were the thousands of college students who came for the war protests fairly portrayed by the media?

7. How are Vietnam War protesters portrayed in movies such as

Secretariat and *Forrest Gump*?

8. What happened to all the war protesters? Did their experiences change their lives?

9. With all the wars our nation fought in the rest of the 20th century and at the beginning of the 21st, can a case be made that each time, we are repeating the same war in means and goals of the 1960s, but expecting different results?

10. What would happen if our nation put even a fraction of its research and war-making budget into Active Peacemaking? What if we citizens did the same?

APPENDIX C

A Fellowship Proposal

Proposal:
Starting Spanish-English Conversation and Fellowship

Six Themes	Activities
1.) Food:	A Carry-in Meal
2.) Family:	Pictures and Scrapbooking
3.) Health:	Mini-Health Fair with Blood Pressure Check
4.) Shopping:	Dollar Store
5.) Church Service:	Worship
6.) Music:	Praise Band, Singing

Agenda

- Gathering with Refreshments;
  - Presentation of Theme;
- One-to-One Practice Session;
  - Group Activity.

NUMBER ONE

Food — *Alimentos*

1. Set up carry-in dinner, foods labeled, prayer, share food and fellowship, waiting for dessert until after the lesson of the evening.

2. Theme: the importance of food and fellowship. If church-based, a story such as Luke 9:10-17 would show the importance of food to Jesus and how churches carry on the tradition. Translation provided. It could be adapted to other languages.

Then present the following vocabulary words for the evening, having everyone say them aloud:

el pan	the bread
el agua	the water
el café	the coffee
el té	the tea
la leche	the milk
la comida	the dinner
la cena	the supper
el desayuno	the breakfast
el almuerzo	the lunch
la carne	the meat
el pollo	the chicken
la cacerola	the casserole
las verduras	the vegetables
las papas	the potatoes
el arroz	the rice
la pasta	the pasta

knife

la fruta	the fruit
la ensalada	the salad
el postre	the dessert
el pastel	the pie, the cake
un plato	a plate
los vasos	the glasses
los tenedores	the forks
las cucharas	the spoons
las servilletas	the napkins
Español	Spanish
Inglés	English

3. One-to-one, practice conversation session, pairing a native Spanish speaker with a native English speaker, or someone fluent in each language.

Vamos a comer.	Let's eat.
Vamos a dar gracias.	Let's say the blessing.
Tome un plato, por favor.	Take a plate, please.
¿Qué desea usted para comer?	What do you want to eat?
El pollo, la ensalada, y el pan	Chicken, salad, and bread
¿Y después?	And then?
Después tomaré postre.	Then I will get dessert.
¿Qué prefiere usted de postre?	What do you prefer for dessert?
Quiero probar todos los postres.	I want to try all the desserts.
Yo deseo fruta y pastel.	I want fruit and pie.

¿Tomará usted té?	Will you take tea?
No, prefiero un vaso de leche.	No, I prefer a glass of milk.
Yo voy a tomar café.	I will drink coffee.
Muchas gracias.	Thank you very much.
De nada.	You're welcome.

4. Help yourselves to dessert with your conversation partner, using the vocabulary and the practice conversation.

5. Assignment for next week: Bring pictures and photographs of your family.

NUMBER TWO
Family *La Familia*

1. Informal time for greeting one another, with coffee, tea, and some homemade cookies or sweets. Name tags will be helpful. Theme: The family, special importance in Hispanic culture and also in the USA.

2. Then present the following vocabulary words for the evening, having everyone say them aloud:

el padre	the father
la madre	the mother
el hijo	the son
la hija	the daughter
el niño	the child (masculine)
la niña	the child (feminine)
la esposa	the wife

el esposo	the husband
el primo	the cousin (masculine)
la prima	the cousin (feminine)
el cuñado	the brother-in-law
la cuñada	the sister-in-law
el tío	the uncle
la tía	the aunt
el abuelo	the grandfather
la abuela	the grandmother
el hermano	the brother
la hermana	the sister
el hombre	the man
la mujer	the woman
el muchacho	the boy
la muchacha	the girl
la boda	the wedding
la quinceañera	the 15th birthday presentation party
álbum de fotografías	scrapbook, photo album
dónde	where
quién	who
cuál	which

Present the articles:

yo	I
usted	you (formal)
tu	you (familiar)
el	he
ella	she
nosotros	we

ustedes	you all (formal)
vosotros	you all (familiar)
ellos	they
su	your
esto, esta	this
mi	my

3. One-to-one practice conversation session, pairing a native Spanish speaker with a native English speaker, or someone fluent in each language. Use the pictures that were brought to class as you practice.

¿Quién es ella?	Who is she?
Ella es mi tía.	She is my aunt.
¿Quién es él?	Who is he?
El es mi abuelo.	He is my grandfather.
¿Es su familia?	Is this your family?
Sí, esta es mi familia.	Yes, this is my family.
Esta es mi esposa.	This is my wife.
Este es mi esposo.	This is my husband.
Es mi hija.	She is my daughter.
Es mi hijo.	He is my son.
¿Cuál es su madre?	Which one is your mother?
¿Cuál es su padre?	Which one is your father?
¿Donde está su familia?	Where is your family?

4. Finish the evening with a scrapbooking demonstration by someone in the congregation that has prepared a display of his or her artistic creations.

NUMBER THREE
Health: *Salud*

1. Informal time for greeting one another, with coffee, tea, and some homemade cookies or sweets. Name tags will be helpful.

2. Theme: the importance of health and wholeness. If church-based, a story such as Matthew 14:34-36 shows the importance to Jesus, and how churches have carried on Jesus' ministry of healing by building hospitals. Translation provided.

Then present the following 25-27 vocabulary words for the evening, having everyone say them aloud:

health exam	*examen de salud*
illness	*enfermedad*
a fever	*una fiebre*
take your pulse	*tomar el pulso*
what hurts?	*¿dónde le duele?*
your blood pressure	*la presión*
your height	*la estatura*
your weight	*el peso*
the thermometer	*el termómetro*
the prescription	*la receta*
a pill	*una píldora*
the clinic	*la clínica*
the hospital	*el hospital*
the doctor's office	*la oficina del médico*
the nurse	*la enfermera*

the technician	*el técnico*
the dietitian	*la dietista*
the dentist	*el dentista*
an appointment	*una cita*
a vaccination	*una vacuna*
flu	*influenza*
health insurance	*seguro de salud*
free	*gratis*
charity	*beneficencia*
dizzy	*mareado*
nauseated	*nauseado*
to feel tired	*sentir cansado*

3. One-to-one practice conversation session, pairing a native Spanish speaker with a native English speaker, or someone fluent in each language. This will be a practice conversation about health.

How are you?	*¿Cómo está?*
How do you feel?	*¿Cómo le siente?*
I am sick.	*Estoy enfermo/enferma.*
I am tired.	*Estoy cansado/cansada.*
I am dizzy.	*Estoy mareado/mareada.*
Do you have a fever?	*¿Tiene usted fiebre?*
I feel well.	*Estoy bien.*
Thank you.	*Gracias.*
Would you like your blood pressure checked?	*¿Se puede chequear la presión?*
Yes, I would, thank you.	*Sí, se puede, gracias.*

4. Introduce the parish nurse or a nurse from the community hospital, who will explain why it is important to get your blood pressure checked regularly. Then people may have their blood pressure checked. If there are other health services available, they may be explained and people invited to participate.

5. Take time to plan the rest of the meeting topics. Class members will work together and carry them out as multicultural field trips and activities.

There are three remaining themes: shopping, church service, and music. These can be planned by native English speakers and native Spanish speakers working together, and carried out more informally. The focus will change from prepared instruction modules to individual class members working together as a team. If class members continue to learn twenty-five new words per session, they will have a 150 new words in their bilingual vocabulary and will be able to use them in simple conversation around six topics.

APPENDIX D

A Contemporary Trip to Discover One's African Roots

When my former coworker and friend, Laura A.M. Johnson, returned from her second year in Africa, I asked if she would allow me to use certain email missives in this book and she also agreed to share her pictures with a group of coworkers who still get together every year. Following is a recreation of her presentation to us that day about three years ago.

Welcome, friends. *Amasaganaleu*! That's Amharic for thank you. Thank you for coming! This past year I've had the best experience of my life. I'll never be the same again. I finally got to be in Africa, the land of my ancestors.

It was an amazing opportunity to be a volunteer for two years in Africa. I'll begin the slide show with Kidist, Justin, and myself on a trip to West Africa with the sky blue ocean behind us. Don't our smiles reveal complete happiness? Justin is my second son for those of you who don't know him. He came to visit me and fell in love with a young lady named Kidist. He was hoping he could bring her to Chicago with him, but things aren't that easy. There's a mountain of paperwork when it comes to immigration and there're delays you wouldn't believe.

The shoreline and the beaches are beautiful as you can see. We spent hours just watching the tide roll in and out and wading through the warm foam. To stand on the shores of the Atlantic, the ocean that our ancestors crossed is spine-tingling. I have become painfully aware that West Africa is where most if not all of our African ancestors came from, from coastal tribes that are still there in today's Senegal, Sierra Leone, Guinea, Liberia. I said a prayer of thanks for the ancestors who sacrificed so much, but were strong enough to survive.

The next picture is of us eating the most delicious shrimp meal I ever ate. Seafood was fresh and cheap. We would go to the shore of the Atlantic Ocean and buy as much as we wanted, and they cleaned it and cooked it for us right there. Here's another picture of food. I tried all kinds of West African foods, including pig's feet, yup! Pig's feet stew. Stews could be made of lots of local foods, like crab, chicken, okra, potato, cassava leaves, onions, and chili peppers. Another meal was whole fried tilapia with rice. They eat rice with everything. Doesn't that sound like good southern cooking?

My job for two years was volunteer college teacher in Ethiopia through the International Foundation for Education and Self Help, an international exchange program started by the late great Doctor Leon Sullivan. Adama University is in a city called Nazareth, which is about a hundred miles from Addis Ababa, the capital of Ethiopia. I hope I served Africa well. I am blessed that I was able to be there and carry out a couple of unique assignments.

My main assignment was to the School of Pedagogy, the Psychology Department. I taught Guidance and Counseling in the Master's Degree program. Here's a picture of the nineteen students, all career counselors in the Ethiopian School System, all men. This next picture is of some of the young ladies I got to know. There weren't any female graduate students, but there were a number of young women attending undergraduate college. I felt they needed encouragement and support, so I sponsored a Girls' Club as an extracurricular activity. It turned out I spent a lot of time with the girls, because their needs were so great. It was a big surprise to me how many of them told me they started out in primary school pretending they were 'boys.' Their parents dressed them for school as boys until the age of twelve when the truth came out: they were actually girls. Can anyone guess the reason they went through all that? There was not enough room for all the children who wanted to go to school. Any openings in primary schools would be filled first by boys. And I learned that if anyone got sick for any length of time, they lost their place in school. Someone else would take their place.

Many of you who know me are aware that most of my adult life I wanted to travel to Africa. My fellow white teachers knew what country their ancestors came from, but not me and my fellow black teachers. It became an obsession for me. I studied African history. I collected pictures of African men and women in a scrapbook, organizing them by country or by tribe. I studied hair, eyes, noses, face shapes, body shapes, trying to identify prototypes of different tribes and cultures. But I knew nothing would take the place of going there. With one son out of college, I knew I would soon have the time and freedom to go. What I lacked was the money. It was then that my husband—bless his heart—offered to give me his savings account. He suggested that one day soon, the opportunity would present itself for me to go. We studied my retirement options, and determined the year I'd be eligible for full retirement. From then on, the doors started opening. I applied and was accepted in the Leon Sullivan program. As a volunteer, I worked for two years for no pay but they provided airfare and housing. That was the biggest part. Does anyone have any questions?

How did you decide to go to Ethiopia?

I didn't choose Ethiopia. It chose me. You may have heard of Haile Selassie, the emperor of Ethiopia. Anyway, he was in power since 1930, and he started a number of reforms in 1966. That's when Leon Sullivan started working with them to create this cultural exchange. It gave me the opportunity to be on the African continent. Even though Ethiopia is way up in the northeast corner, I was there in Africa in real life.

What was it like living day to day in a third-world country?

I lived in a little clay block house. Ethiopia's going through a drought. We were without water and electricity for days at a time, because we had no rain. That meant no refrigeration. I learned to shop on a daily basis—just enough for the day. The lights were out every three days, from six o'clock to nine o'clock at night. I would usually go out for dinner with other teachers on those nights and return just as the lights were coming back on. It worked out well. Otherwise, I just stayed at home alone, napping in the dark. I knew when the power was back on, because the fan came on and sent blessed cool breezes over me. "Aha, let there be light," I would say and then roll over and go back to sleep. The power went back off at six o'clock in the morning, so I got up at five o'clock to iron what I was going to wear and charge up my camera. That was conservation to the max. The bigger picture was difficult: when there was no water, then there was no power, therefore, fewer jobs. Factories closed; spigots were dry; since farmers couldn't water their crops, there were few fresh vegetables in the market, except those drought-resistant ones that tasted more like cardboard than spinach. Children were thirsty and hungry. Everything was dusty. We prayed, Give us this day our daily bread and we meant it literally.

Did you see a lot of poverty?

On a daily basis I witnessed people suffering. I saw children begging for bread, mothers begging for coins. There were so many people who had afflictions due to polio and malnutrition dragging their bodies in and out of traffic, begging. One time, while sitting in a traffic jam, I saw a young woman, no more than twenty years old, wearing a plastic sack—a sack that maybe flour or onions had been transported in. I could see her naked body through large gaping holes in the sack. She wore no shoes. She was going through a heap of garbage, looking for I don't know what. I couldn't help but wonder what would happen to this girl with no clothing, no food, no nothing. I instantly whispered a prayer for her and was upset that I didn't have enough presence of mind to have the taxi driver stop, so I could try to help her. It came to me that if I had a Ziploc bag with clean clothing, it would've been so nice to give her some, maybe a life saver. I promised myself that if I'm able to return to Ethiopia, I will bring some bags of provisions and carry one with me at all times for any woman in her situation.

She wiped a tear from her eye. "These were some of the adjustments I had to make when I went to serve in what we call a developing country. Yet and still, I want you to know that these two years were the most satisfying years in my entire life—what a ride!

What were some of the problems the girls had in preparing for a better life?

I put out the good old question box for every meeting of the Girls' Club, and found Ethiopian girls had many of the same questions as Chicago girls—about boys and relationships and sex. So I did a series of workshops for young women on campus addressing basic human sexuality and decision-making.

I don't want to give the wrong impression. The girls were very serious about their studies. Most of the girls traveled from the rural areas of Ethiopia to Adama University to receive a college education. They weren't usually supported or encouraged by their parents because most families believed a girl shouldn't be trained to be a competitor on the global arena or in the home, but rather she should be a good housewife—period. These girls came to school with a shopping bag holding all their worldly possessions. Yet they were determined to learn, and were existing on nothing more than the essentials of life. I assisted as many of them as I could. One thing I did was provide a bus ticket and a few dollars for meals so some of them could travel home for Christmas and Easter holidays.

Christmas and Easter? Are there Christians in Ethiopia?

Oh, yes. The university students were about half Christian (Coptic, Ethiopian Orthodox) and half Muslim. In all of Ethiopia, the population is about one-third Christian, one-third Muslim, and one-third traditional or indigenous religions. The different religions get along fine. I don't know how they do it, achieve such tolerance, but Ethiopia should be a model for other countries.

For example, my Bible study group. The problem for me was finding an English-speaking church. Therefore I couldn't go to church every Sunday, so I started a Bible study group for expatriates in our community. We met at my home, once a week. This midweek fellowship was very inspirational and a blessing to me. In our group were four Koreans, two East Indians, three Filipinos, and myself. I'll give you one neat story about a South Korean brother, Ryu, who brought his guitar. He spoke very little English and said he knew nothing but praise songs in English. One time we encouraged him to teach us a song in his native tongue. He began singing one, and I was aware instantly that I knew the tune and began singing it in English. I told them that in my home church we sing this very same song every Sunday—'we worship you, hallelujah, hallelujah, we worship you for who you are. You are good all the time; all the time you are good.' We had so much fun, Ryu singing in Korean and me in English, the very same song, same rhythm.

A Filipino sister started beating my souvenir bongo drums, and I started clapping and dancing. Pretty soon everyone joined in and we had an amazing time! Just think, all over the world God's children are singing his praises, from the Alps to the Serengeti, and the African plains, across the Middle East and Asia, from the top of the world to the bottom, all seven continents, in every tongue and vernacular. Hallelujah! Blessed are those who love God and can worship him freely.

However, just next door to Ethiopia is the Sudan. Christians there are persecuted daily because of their beliefs. When I came back home, my grandson asked me, "Grandma, do you think you made a difference in Africa?" I had to answer him, "I'm not sure, child, but Africa sure made a difference in Grandma!"

Did you ever get an answer to your question about where your ancestors came from? Was it a country in West Africa?

I have to tell one more amazing story to answer you honestly. I had to drive a hundred miles to the closest English-speaking church. One Sunday I went to that church for an international potluck dinner. There were more than one thousand five-hundred Christians present from fifty-eight different countries. We had Russians, Cubans, Danes, Australians, Pakistanis, African people from countries all over West, North and East Africa, also Yemen, Saudi Arabia, Europe, and of course, the USA. I was the only African American in attendance. The potluck dinner was out of this world! Then there were tents where countries had displays and served more goodies. The West Africans (Nigeria, Ghana, Malawi, Senegal, Gambia, Togo, Benin, Mali, Cote D'Ivoire, and Sierra Leone) all shared the same tent. It was at this gathering in the West African tent that I received clear visual confirmation that my ancestors were West African.

The food in particular was like a Thanksgiving feast at Big Mama's. Sweet potato pie, corn casserole, corn meal muffins, mashed turnips, turnovers. I felt completely at home with this group. I'm determined to make my next trip to West Africa. I'm going to start with Sierra Leone where two of the church women invited me to visit and continue my search for my ancestors.

I just want to finish by saying to you that there's a big world out there. You've heard of the "seven wonders of the world." I happen to believe there are a lot more than seven. Countries all over the world are populated by regular friendly people like you and me. Most people just want to live in peace and make a good life for themselves and their families. Some people have dreams and want to do big things; thank God for those who make this a better world for all of us. I want to challenge you to travel outside Chicago to some other place if you possibly can. Join the Peace Corps or organize a mission trip from your church. If everyone would make just one attempt to get to know and understand people who live genuinely differently from you, all these stupid wars would end. We would have world peace. Yes, we would. Most of all, follow your heart; together we will build a better, more peaceful world.